THE MIRACLE OF MENTORING

A BIBLICAL GUIDE TO SPIRITUAL FATHERING

by
Bayless Conley

Harrison House
Tulsa, Oklahoma

05 04 03 02 01   10 09 08 07 06 05 04 03 02 01

The Miracle of Mentoring—
A Biblical Guide to Spiritual Fathering
ISBN 1-57794-452-6
Copyright © 2001 by Bayless Conley
Cottonwood Christian Center
P.O. Box 486
Los Alamitos, California 90720

Published by Harrison House, Inc.
P.O. Box 35035
Tulsa, Oklahoma 74153

CONTENTS

There are a lot of people around who can't wait to tell you
what you've done wrong, but there aren't many fathers willing
to take the time and effort to help you grow up.

1 Cor. 4:15 MESSAGE

INTRODUCTION

One of the great tragedies in the world today is the lack of true father figures, mentors whose lives serve as a pattern for the younger generation—not just those who train, coach, and give out instruction, but those who model the art of successful living. Without the example of a father, children are at a disadvantage. They are forced to make decisions and choose pathways that their own wisdom and experience have not prepared them for. Mistakes, heartache, and regret—most of which could have been avoided—are the results.

Not only is the lack of a father's example and guiding hand evident in society today, but it has also taken its toll in the church. This is what the apostle Paul was referring to when he said, "For though you might have ten thousand instructors in Christ, yet you do not have many fathers..." (1 Cor. 4:15).

This book has been written to address this issue of fatherless Christianity. It is my intention to inspire this generation of Christians to rise to the occasion and assume the responsibility of mentoring their children as fathers in the Lord.

A number of years ago I attended a convention in a nearby state. After the evening meeting I retired to my room, where I began to earnestly pray about the scarcity of spiritual fathers in the church. Although I had been blessed with several mature believers who greatly contributed to my own spiritual growth, I personally had been grappling with the fact that I didn't have a true spiritual father in my own life.

As I prayed, I was seized with such a sense of grief that I began to weep before the Lord. This went on for some time, and though I found comfort and encouragement, I still left that place with a sense of needing some sort of mentor.

Some time later as I was once again lamenting how few spiritual fathers there are today in the body of Christ, I sensed the Holy Spirit challenging me as He spoke to my heart. He said, "It's time for you to stop looking for a father in the Lord and start being one." I now pass on that challenge to you.

Will you give yourself to the self-sacrifice to which all fathers are called? Will you lay down your life, making mentoring your children your main purpose in life? I challenge you to say yes to this high calling and to approach the following chapters as God's resource for your calling.

SPIRITUAL FATHERING

I do not write these things to shame you, but as my beloved children I warn you. For though you might have ten thousand instructors in Christ, yet you do not have many fathers; for in Christ Jesus I have begotten you through the gospel. Therefore I urge you, imitate me. For this reason I have sent Timothy to you, who is my beloved and faithful son in the Lord, who will remind you of my ways in Christ, as I teach everywhere in every church.

1 Corinthians 4:14-17

Today, as in Paul's day, no one has trouble finding instructors—they are a dime a dozen. In fact, the Scripture declares that in the last days people will heap up teachers for themselves. (2 Tim. 4:3.) Folks will line up to be imparters of information. But to find a true father in the faith is a rare thing, indeed. A father imparts more than information. A father imparts himself. He becomes vulnerable. He sacrifices for his sons and daughters. He watches over his children in prayer and rejoices in their progress. He carries them in his heart. And he has "…no greater joy than to hear that [his] children walk in truth" (3 John 1:4). It takes commitment to be a father.

THE PRINCIPLE OF SPIRITUAL FATHERING IS FOR BOTH MEN AND WOMEN

Before proceeding any further, let me state that the principle of spiritual fathering or mentoring is not just for men. This truth applies to women in the body of Christ just as much as it does to men, because mentoring is basically being a spiritual parent to someone who is younger in the Lord. Paul declares in Galatians 3:28, "...there is neither male nor female; for you are all one in Christ Jesus." The idea is that members of the church, whether male or female, as they mature in the Lord, take someone who is younger and more inexperienced in spiritual matters and begin to mentor him or her into maturity. In fact, Paul exhorted the older women to teach the younger women. (Titus 2:3,4.)

So, ladies, please keep in mind that even though we will predominantly be using the masculine term of "fathering" through-out this book, the principle applies equally to men and women.

THE FIRST THING FATHERS DO

The first thing fathers do is produce children. Natural fathers produce physical children, and spiritual fathers produce spiritual children. Notice the language of 1 Corinthians 4:14-17: "my beloved children" (v.14); "I have begotten you" (v.15); "my beloved and faithful son" (v.17). So people become spiritual fathers, first of all, by winning people to Christ through sharing the gospel! Paul said, "...in Christ Jesus I have begotten you through the gospel" (v. 15).

Jesus explained this same truth to Nicodemus in John, 3, when He said, "...You must be born again." Yet in order for the Holy Spirit to accomplish that work of regeneration, there must always be a certain element present in a person's life in order for the new birth to come about. The Holy Spirit needs something to work with: the seed of God's Word! First Peter 1:23 says, "having been born again, not of corruptible seed but incorruptible, through the word of God

2

which lives and abides forever." You must sow the seed of the Word if people are to be born again. People are "begotten through the gospel," as Paul said in 1 Corinthians 4:15.

Spiritual fathers sow seeds just as natural fathers do! If your wife gets pregnant, you are not going to wonder how it happened. You know how it happened! To expect people to be saved (birthed spiritually) without planting the seed of the Word in their hearts is like a husband and wife praying for a baby and never sharing sexual intimacy! Human beings can only become natural parents through the act of planting seeds. And we can only become spiritual parents through the act of planting incorruptible seeds.

SEEDS, SOIL, AND STYROFOAM CUPS

Years ago my oldest son, Harrison, came home from church with a styrofoam cup filled with soil. His Sunday school teacher had been telling the children about how God's Word works as a seed does, and that in order for it to grow and produce the things it promises, we must first plant it in our hearts. The kids had all planted seeds in their cups and were told to take them home, set them in a window sill, water them regularly, and watch them grow. Harrison was excited as he told me what he learned in class. As his teacher had instructed, we watered the seed and set the cup in the window. The next morning Harrison raced to the kitchen to look at his cup, but to his disappointment, nothing was growing.

"Dad, let's dig it up. It's not working!" he exclaimed.

"Give it time," I responded. "Seeds need time to grow."

Every day we went through the same routine.

"Dad, it's not working! Let's dig it up and see what's wrong."

My repeated response was, "Give it time. If we dig it up, we'll kill the seed." But after two weeks, curiosity got the better of me, so I called Harrison and said, "It should have grown by now. Let's dig it up."

We poured all the dirt out of the cup on the kitchen table and methodically went through it with our fingers. I kept thinking, *Where is the seed? Where is the seed?*

"Harrison, there is no seed in here," I said.

He smiled and said, "I guess I forgot to plant it."

We had a good laugh and tossed the cup and the soil into the trash. The moral is this: You can't expect a plant to grow where no seed has been sown—and you can't expect a person to be saved if the seed of God's Word has not been planted.

SALVATION SEEDS

I was saved because of the seeds planted by a twelve-year-old boy. I had looked for the truth but could never seem to find it. I went from religion to religion and from cult to cult, all the while experimenting with drugs in my quest for life's meaning. But I always came up empty. Then one day a twelve-year-old boy came up to me in a park and told me about Jesus. He shared the gospel with me and told me of God's plan of salvation. I wasn't ready at that moment to receive, but the seeds of my salvation had been planted.

Shortly thereafter, I moved to the sprawling metropolis of Mexico City. I was living with a friend, indulging in everything I always thought might make me happy, yet I was miserable. There was no lack of money, drugs, alcohol, or sex, yet I was constantly bothered on the inside by something I couldn't explain.

Those gospel seeds that the young boy had planted in me several months earlier were beginning to germinate and grow. I sat night after night staring out the window from our high-rise apartment, looking over the sea of lights that, at that time, represented eleven million people living in Mexico's capital city. I thought about my life. I thought about the young boy's words. I thought about Jesus. Then one day I did it—I left. I told my partner I was leaving and going back to the United States.

"When?" he asked.

"Tomorrow," I replied. And that was it.

In the morning I was on my way—3,000 miles back to the city of Ashland, Oregon, to find the twelve-year-old boy who had told me about Christ. And find him I did! I was born again within a few weeks—because the incorruptible seed of God's Word had been planted in my heart!

First Corinthians 3:5-9 says:

> **Who then is Paul, and who is Apollos, but ministers through whom you believed, as the Lord gave to each one? I planted, Apollos watered, but God gave the increase. So then neither he who plants is anything, nor he who waters, but God who gives the increase. Now he who plants and he who waters are one, and each one will receive his own reward according to his own labor. For we are God's fellow workers; you are God's field, you are God's building.**

God gives the increase, but the seed must be sown! God gets the glory, but the seed must be sown! God gives the reward, but the seed must be sown! Someone may come along and water the plant. Someone else may come along and thrust in the sickle and reap. But none of this can happen without the planting of a seed.

Years ago I planted a macadamia nut tree in our front yard. The gardener later put in a sprinkler system that watered it, and it eventually became a large, healthy tree that produced lots of delicious nuts. We eventually sold our house to a friend, and now he gets to harvest all those tasty nuts! I planted, the gardener watered, and now my friend gets the pleasure of harvesting and enjoying the crop. The same process often occurs in spiritual harvesting. Sometimes the same person does it all—planting, watering, and harvesting. But usually, as with my macadamia nut tree, several people are involved in a person's conversion.

We find Jesus teaching this same truth to His disciples in John 4:35-38:

> "Do you not say, 'There are still four months and then comes the harvest'? Behold, I say to you, lift up your eyes and look at the fields, for they are already white for harvest! And he who reaps receives wages, and gathers fruit for eternal life, that both he who sows and he who reaps may rejoice together. For in this the saying is true: 'One sows and another reaps.' I sent you to reap that for which you have not labored; others have labored, and you have entered into their labors."

Shortly after my conversion to Christ, I was busy sharing the gospel with everyone I knew—and many I didn't know. I wanted the whole world to experience this wonderful relationship I had with Jesus. But more than anyone else, I wanted my family, to be saved. I hadn't seen them in years, and all they knew of me was my former days as a drug user and alcoholic. It was not the happiest of reunions, mostly because I was filled with zeal and void of wisdom. I preached to both of my parents and my sister relentlessly.

Although my mom and sister were somewhat open to the gospel, my father didn't seem to be open at all. In fact, one afternoon he bluntly announced to me that he'd liked me better when I'd been on drugs! (I think that gives you an idea of how overbearing I was in sharing Christ.) What was I going to do? My dad wasn't responding, and I felt that the entire job of planting and harvesting his spiritual conversion was resting on my shoulders.

During this time, I was volunteering at a local ministry, answering phone calls. One day as I was busy on the phone, a woman I had never seen before walked up to me and after reading my name badge she very deliberately said, "Bayless Conley. Does your dad have the same name as you?"

"Yes, ma'am," I responded.

"Praise God!" she exclaimed. "I have been witnessing to your dad for months, and every week at our ladies prayer group we pray for his salvation."

I was stunned. It was as if God said, "You don't need to worry about your dad. It's not all resting on your shoulders. I care about him more than you do, and I have the whole body of Christ to use as a resource in reaching him."

A few months later my dad was saved, Spirit-filled, and is now a faithful member of my church. One sows, and another reaps.

Here is a portion of a letter I received that illustrates this same truth:

I don't know the exact date when I passed through the living room and your TV ministry caught my attention. I watched it and felt that Jesus was pointing His finger at me. You said, "You are not watching this show by accident, but by divine guidance." I couldn't explain my feelings. After that, I tuned in to your show every Sunday I could and decided to try and put God first in my life.

One day I was driving to work and saw a guy walking the same direction, carrying a Bible. I thought as I passed by, "Should I give him a ride?" It turns out that he had just started at my work place and took the bus most of the way. When he came into my office (he was a custodian), he asked me if I knew Jesus and if I was saved. For a couple of days, he ministered to me, and I felt the conviction of the Holy Spirit. He invited me to his church in Norwalk, California. Remembering what you had said—"Get to your local church and invite Jesus into your life"—I did! I felt the power of Christ in the church and was overwhelmed. I knew that Christ was there for me through the good and bad times of my life. I quickly received Him and was saved, and then I told my wife. She too was saved, and so were my sister and her husband and a couple of friends. Today I am in awe of what Christ can do and has already done! My life is awesome with Jesus, and I love Him very much.

> *P.S. I thank God and you for our salvation. Could you help me pray for my father and brothers' salvation too? Thanks, Pastor!*

Love, Everette and Valerie

We sowed, another watered, and the minister from the church in Norwalk, California, reaped the harvest!

SEEDS TAKE TIME TO GROW

If you sow a seed and see no immediate results, don't get discouraged. A farmer doesn't get discouraged after he sows his field. He rejoices because he knows that as surely as he put that seed in the ground, a harvest is coming! If you share Christ with people and no one responds, you are not a failure! You are doing what is necessary to bring a harvest. There is power in the seed, but that power is not unlocked until you put the seed in the ground. If no one plants the seed, a harvest is impossible!

Think about the words of Jesus in Mark 4:14,30-32:

> **The sower sows the word.**
>
> **To what shall we liken the kingdom of God? Or with what parable shall we picture it? It is like a mustard seed which, when it is sown on the ground, is smaller than all the seeds on earth; but when it is sown, it grows up and becomes greater than all herbs, and shoots out large branches, so that the birds of the air may nest under its shade.**

When it is sown, it grows! Contained in a tiny mustard seed is the entire blueprint for the plant. Its shape, color, and fragrance are all locked inside the seed. But when it is sown, that power is unleashed. As it begins to grow, it even pushes rocks out of the way that stand between it and the light of day. It pushes towards the sky, stretches out its branches, and says, "Here I am!"

In the same way, the power of a changed life is locked in the seed of the gospel, and once it hits the soil of a human heart, it goes to work. It pushes sin out of the way and turns a person into a new creature in Christ. And this new creation rises up and says, "Look out, world, here I am! But it's not really me—it's Christ living in me!"

It doesn't matter if you are eloquent when you share the gospel or if you stumble over every word you say. Why? Because the power is in the incorruptible seed, not in your presentation!

My wife's dad is a farmer. He grew up working on a farm, and he eventually raised a family of nine children on his own farm. So he really knows how to make things grow! One might say he is an expert at farming. But do you know what? The seeds he plants will just as surely grow for me as they will for him. If we stood side by side in the field, planting seeds—Elmer in his overalls and work boots, and I in a suit and street shoes—the seeds I would be planting wouldn't say, "Wait a minute! This guy putting us in the ground doesn't have overalls on! He's no farmer! And look at those shoes he is wearing! He's from the city! We're not going to grow for him!"

No, friend, seeds are no respecter of persons. They will grow for me just as they will grow for the career farmer.

PLANT SOME SEEDS

The same is true of spiritual farming. You don't have to be a career pastor, evangelist, prophet, apostle, or teacher to sow and grow God's spiritual seed. So share the gospel with someone. In your own way and with your own personality, plant some seeds. You may not be as polished or as eloquent in your presentation as someone else, but by all means, get some seeds in the ground.

I was doing some meetings recently in Australia, and one morning during some free time, I walked over to a local beach to do some jogging. As I was running along the water's edge, I passed a young man who looked as if he had spent the night on the beach, and I had a distinct impression that I needed to talk to him. As I turned back, I noticed that his hair was matted and full of sand and that he most likely had passed out from too much drinking the previous night. I had no speech prepared—nothing was premeditated. I simply walked up to him, introduced myself, and told him of my impression to talk to him. I spent about five minutes sharing my testimony. I told him how Jesus could change his life and what he needed to do in order to be saved. He was open and respectful, but he wasn't ready at that time to give his life to Christ. So off I went. Seed planted. Mission accomplished.

God will send another to water and another to harvest, and who knows? That young man with the matted, sand-filled hair may turn out to be a "nation shaker" for Christ. After all, who would have thought that when a twelve-year-old boy shared Christ in a park one day with a long-haired, drugged-out hippie that he would end up being a pastor? But here I am!

The first step in being a spiritual father is sowing seeds. So share with your family and relatives. Share with your neighbors. Share with your co-workers. Share with strangers. Don't wait for conditions to be perfect. Many don't plant the seeds of the gospel because they are waiting for "perfect conditions." Ecclesiastes 11:4-6 talks about this:

> **He who observes the wind will not sow, and he who regards the clouds will not reap. As you do not know what is the way of the wind, or how the bones grow in the womb of her who is with child, so you do not know the works of God who makes everything. In the morning sow your seed, and in the evening do not withhold your hand; for you do not know which will prosper, either this or that, or whether both alike will be good.**

These verses paint the picture of an incredible truth that we must understand. First, we must sow our seed at all times, whether or not conditions seem favorable. Wind or no wind, clouds or no clouds, morning, afternoon, or evening—don't withhold your hand. Sow the gospel seeds that have been entrusted to you. "Cast your bread upon the waters…. Give a serving to seven, and also to eight…" (vv. 1,2). The result will be new births! Spiritual children!

Ecclesiastes 11:5 says, "As you do not know what is the way of the wind, or how the bones grow in the womb of her who is with child, so you do not know the works of God who makes everything." This is the verse Jesus was referring to when He spoke to Nicodemus about being born again in John 3:8. We may not know the way of the wind—where it comes from or where it goes—but we will see the work of regeneration accomplished by God's Spirit when we sow our seed and share with others!

Spiritual fathers sow. The more seed you sow and the more often you sow, the greater the harvest will be. "He who sows sparingly will also reap sparingly, and he who sows bountifully will also reap bountifully" (2 Cor. 9:6).

Carry tracts and pass them out. In your own way, share your personal story of how you came to faith in Christ. Share a Bible verse with someone. Invite people to come to church so they can hear the gospel. With some, you will "sow and go." You'll sow the seed, go your way, and God will have others tend to the results. But with others, you'll "sow and grow." You'll stay with them and help them to grow in Christ. You will be a spiritual father or mother to them.

TEARS AND WEEPING

Along with planting the seed through the act of sharing, there is another important aspect in this arena of spiritual fathering: prayer. *You will be more successful if you talk to God about men before you talk to men about God.* Scattering God's seed prayerlessly is not as effective as scattering it prayerfully. The psalmist says, "Those who sow in tears shall reap in joy. He who continually goes forth weeping, bearing seed for sowing, shall doubtless come again with rejoicing, bringing his sheaves with him" (Ps. 126:5,6).

Always pray for direction as to where and how you should plant your seed. But, more importantly, let the Holy Spirit fill you with a sense of the desperate condition people are in without Christ. This is a condition worth weeping and laboring in prayer over, even as the apostle Paul said in Galatians 4:19, "My little children, for whom I labor in birth again until Christ is formed in you." He had agonized in prayer for their salvation, and now he agonizes again for their maturity.

People are not born again without the incorruptible seed of God's Word being sown in their lives and someone laboring over them in prayer. And spiritual fathers do both.

You are not reading this book today by some coincidence. This moment has been bathed in someone's tears. Someone has prayed for you. Someone has labored in the Spirit for you, believing that the incorruptible seed of God's Word will penetrate your heart—either to bring you to Christ or to bring you to maturity in Christ.

By the way, as I shared with the young man on the beach that day, he blurted out, "My mom's a Christian, and she's told me about Jesus." At that moment, I knew that her prayers had brought me across his path and that the precious seed I was sowing into his life would doubtless result in a harvest. I pray that when he does respond, he will find a father in the Lord who will take him under his wing and help him to grow.

AS FATHERS GO, SO GO THE CHILDREN

For though you might have ten thousand instructors in Christ, yet you do not have many fathers.

1 Corinthians 4:15

Fathers, like instructors, teach by precept, but they do more than that. Through example, they impart their character to their children and, in the process, reproduce children in their own image.

Then God said, "Let Us make man in Our image, according to Our likeness."

And Adam lived one hundred and thirty years, and begot a son in his own likeness, after his image and named him Seth.

Genesis 1:26; 5:3

When God made humans, He created them not only in His likeness but also in His image. In my interpretation of the word, *likeness* refers to physical appearance, but I believe *image* refers to inward nature and character. So after creating man, God gave Adam His same ability. When his son Seth was born, he was not just physically the "likeness" of Adam; he also grew into his "image," adopting his inward character and habits of life. This happens by example and is undoubtedly the most powerful force that a spiritual (or natural) father has at his disposal to shape the lives of his children.

"...I have begotten you through the gospel. Therefore I urge you, imitate me" (1 Cor. 4:15,16). The father purposely teaches by example, not just by precept. "Timothy, my son...will remind you of my way of life in Christ Jesus, which agrees with what I teach everywhere in every church" (1 Cor. 4:17 NIV). Paul said, "My life and my teaching agree!" To be a true father in the Lord, this is essential.

Think about parents who say to their children, "Do as I say, not as I do." Children generally do as their parents say when they are in their parents' presence, but they do as their parents do when they are not being observed. I can see myself in all three of my children, which is both rewarding and sobering! They unconsciously follow the example that I set for them!

All of my children are involved in different athletic activities, so as a family, we spend a lot of time at baseball games, soccer matches, etc. On occasion, while attending one of these events, we witness someone's child swearing at an umpire and throwing things because he doesn't agree with a call that has been made. And invariably, if you wait awhile, you will also see the father doing the same thing because that is generally how the boy learned it. He has just grown up into the "image" of his father by following his example.

In Acts 7:51, Stephen told the Jews, "...as your fathers did, so do you." According to Ezekiel, Israel ended in spiritual ruin because "...their eyes were fixed on their fathers' idols" (Ezek. 20:24). It was true of the people in Ezekiel's day, and it is true of people today.

SPIRITUAL MENTORING

Time and time again, I have seen people following the ways of their spiritual mentors. I have friends in ministry who are incredibly anointed and gifted preachers, but their families are in trouble. Their wives are sorrowing due to neglect. Their children are rebelling and don't want to have anything to do with church because Daddy's idol is the pulpit. These preachers put the pulpit before anything else—even before their relationship with God. Ministry has become their god. They are driven, not led. They have no time for family, and very little time for prayer.

Even if they see that they are in a crisis, it's hard for them to pull back and put life's priorities back into proper order. Like a moth drawn to a flame, they seem irresistibly drawn into the grinding machinery of ministry to the point that they have developed an addiction to ministry. They are, in a sense, workaholics, directing all their energies and drawing their fulfillment from ministry at the expense of the other areas of their lives.

The tragedy is that many times the exact same weaknesses and problems exist in the lives of those who mentored them. Rather than learning from the mistakes of their mentors, they reproduce them. Unfortunately, this even happens in the area of moral failure. *As your fathers did, so do you.* Paul exhorted Titus "...to be sober-minded, in all things showing yourself to be a pattern of good works; in doctrine showing integrity, reverence, incorruptibility..." (Titus 2:6,7). In like manner, he told young Timothy to "...be an example to the believers..." (1 Tim. 4:12). Your life is a blueprint that someone will follow. Whether positive or negative, someone will follow the pattern you set!

People who weren't even aware that I was learning from their examples have shaped much of my own spiritual life. I learned the importance of obedience to God by the example of an old woman named Eva, who, despite the fact that it made her unpopular to some, faithfully shared whatever message God had put in her heart. I learned to trust God for strength by watching another aged saint we called Mom. She was close to eighty years old, and yet she single-handedly raised six orphans, ran a ministry, and had oversight of a small business.

I learned the value of praying in the Spirit (1 Cor. 14:2) by observing a traveling evangelist, whose meetings I drove hundreds of miles to attend. He would arrive several hours early to his meetings, find an isolated spot, and pray until it was time to start the meeting. I learned the power of boldness from the example of a country preacher who, despite the fact that he had no teeth, preached the gospel without apology and boldly prayed for miracles. I learned to live by faith through the example of the young boy who brought me to Christ and his family.

I learned to listen in my heart for God's wisdom from the pastor I served for two years when I first entered ministry. People came to him with the most difficult questions and situations and, time after time, I listened as this profound wisdom flowed from his lips. He had learned the secret of listening to God with the ears of his heart while at the same time listening to people with the ears on his head.

All of these people served as patterns for me, and I owe much to their faithful examples. But what of us? What kind of spiritual blueprints are we laying out for others to follow? Are our lives worthy of imitation?

SERVE AS EXAMPLES IN SEVEN IMPORTANT AREAS

To help you assess where you need to be if your children are to grow up into a godly blueprint of your image, I'm sharing seven areas in which every spiritual father should purposely and consciously serve as examples. These principles will be listed and explained throughout the next few chapters. So get out a highlighter to mark the points and prepare to make some mental notes about where you are now in the process, because I want to help you get to where you need to be.

1. **Be an example by having passion to see the lost come to Christ.**

    ...I myself strive to please [to accommodate myself to the

opinions, desires, and interests of others, adapting myself to] all men in everything I do, not aiming at or considering my own profit and advantage, but that of the many in order that they may be saved.

1 Corinthians 10:33 AMP

Imitate me, just as I also imitate Christ.

1 Corinthians 11:1

Paul says, "Imitate me, as I imitate Christ, who left all and gave up all to save us!" If it costs me money, ease, comfort—even legitimate things that I may be entitled to—I must be willing to give it up. I must be willing to adjust my schedule or my lifestyle, if necessary, if it results in people getting saved!

We cannot afford to have a casual, apathetic attitude about the salvation of the lost. We must be passionate! It is of preeminent importance to God, and it should be to us. It is the reason for which Christ died!

Our attitude will be reproduced in our spiritual children. When we are no longer touched by the plight of lost people and we are no longer actively doing something about bringing them to the Savior, then we are no longer following Jesus, because He said in Matthew 4:19, "Follow Me, and I will make you fishers of men." We need to pray for the lost, give of our finances in order to get the gospel to them, and share Christ with them ourselves.

"DO YOU REALLY WANT TO SEE HIM SAVED?"

A friend of mine was earnestly praying for the salvation of one of his neighbors one evening. God interrupted his prayers and spoke to his heart, saying, "Do you really want to see him saved?"

"Yes, Lord," was my friend's honest response. What came next really put his earnestness to the test.

"Then give him your motorcycle."

There was a long pause, followed by, "Why, Lord?"

"If you really want to see him saved, give him your motorcycle and see what happens."

Without further discussion, my friend rode his motorcycle across the street and into the garage where the neighbor was working. "Do you like my motorcycle?"

"Yeah, sure. Why?"

"It's yours."

"What do you mean, it's mine?"

"It's yours. I'm giving it to you."

"Why would you give me your motorcycle?"

"God wants you to know that He loves you."

At that, the neighbor began to cry. A few minutes later, he was praying the sinner's prayer and receiving Jesus as his Savior.

This man truly lived out Paul's words by accommodating himself to the desires and interests of his neighbor that he might be saved. By his godly example, he was saying, "Imitate me, as I imitate Christ."

2. Be an example by having faith in God.

And we desire that each one of you show the same diligence to the full assurance of hope until the end, that you do not become sluggish, but imitate those who through faith and patience inherit the promises. For when God made a promise to Abraham, because He could swear by no one greater, He swore by Himself, saying, "Surely blessing I will bless you, and multiplying I will multiply you." And so, after he had patiently endured, he obtained the promise.

Hebrews 6:11-15

Abraham is cited as an example of someone who, through faith and patience, inherited a promise. In fact, above all other figures in Scripture, Abraham is set forth as a pattern for faith. Romans 4:12

tells us that we are to "…walk in the steps of the faith which our father Abraham had…."

So if we as fathers and mothers in the Lord are to serve as examples in the area of faith, we must learn to follow the example set by Abraham who, according to Romans 4:16, "…is the father of us all."

> **Therefore it is of faith that it might be according to grace, so that the promise might be sure to all the seed, not only to those who are of the law, but also to those who are of the faith of Abraham, who is the father of us all (as it is written, "I have made you a father of many nations") in the presence of Him whom he believed—God, who gives life to the dead and calls those things which do not exist as though they did; who, contrary to hope, in hope believed, so that he became the father of many nations, according to what was spoken, "So shall your descendants be." And not being weak in faith, he did not consider his own body, already dead (since he was about a hundred years old), and the deadness of Sarah's womb. He did not waver at the promise of God through unbelief, but was strengthened in faith, giving glory to God, and being fully convinced that what He had promised He was also able to perform.**
>
> **Romans 4:16-21**
>
> **And so, after he had patiently endured, he obtained the promise.**
>
> **Hebrews 6:15**

As we study this account of Abraham's faith, four great truths begin to emerge:

- **Abraham called things that did not exist as though they did.** (Rom. 4:17.)

According to Romans 4:17, God first spoke of nonexistent things as though they existed, but Abraham soon followed His example. God told Abraham (who was childless), "I have made you a father of many nations," a seemingly ridiculous declaration, given the existing circumstances. But faith always begins with a declaration from God, because inherent in the promise of God is the power to bring it to pass—if it is believed and acted upon.

In conjunction with God's statement about having made Abraham the father of many nations, He also did something very interesting. He changed Abraham's name, which had previously been Abram, which I've read means "father of height or altitude,"[1] to Abraham, meaning "father of a multitude."[2]

God also changed the name of Sarai to Sarah, which means "princess."[3] From the moment God did that and Abraham accepted it, every time he and Sarah said their names, *they were calling things that did not exist as though they did!*

Imagine the surprise of folks in the camp as Sarah called out to Abraham to come to dinner, and he responded by answering back, "Coming, my princess!" People probably said, "The pressure has finally gotten to them. They wanted a baby so bad that it has sent them off the deep end. Imagine! Calling himself the father of a multitude and his wife a princess! Why, they've never been able to have children, and do they think they are going to start now? He is almost a hundred, and she is ninety! Father of many nations? I don't think so."

But, friend, when God calls something that doesn't exist as though it did, He authorizes us to do the same. This is the way of faith.

Think about God's words to Joshua as he stood before the fortified city of Jericho: "See! I have given Jericho into your hand, its king, and the mighty men of valor" (Josh. 6:2). God was telling Joshua to see it as if it were already done, calling things that didn't exist as though they did! The Lord further proceeded to tell Joshua to shout while the walls were still standing, because only then would the victory he'd already won by faith become a physical reality.

In order to follow in the steps of the faith that our Father Abraham had, we must, based on God's Word, learn to call things that do not exist as though they did.

• **Abraham believed according to what was spoken.** (Rom. 4:18.)

Abraham didn't just wake up one morning and decide to start believing that he would be the father of many nations. It was something that God initiated. God spoke, and Abraham believed according to what was spoken—and the process is the same for us. Faith comes by hearing and hearing by the Word of God. Faith is born from the promises and is sustained by the promises. Without a promise, faith has no foundation—without a promise, faith isn't faith at all.

Whatever kind of situation you may be facing now, these are the first things you should ask yourself: "Has God spoken anything about my situation? Are there any promises in the Bible that cover what I'm going through?" If there are, you can believe those promises and see results. But you must have a promise, because having faith without a promise is like standing on the ocean shore without a ship to sail in. All of your "believing" will get you nowhere.

Once you have found a promise to cover your need, you must anchor your faith on that promise and choose to believe it above all other things. Abraham did. He believed according to what was spoken and not according to how he felt. He believed according to what was spoken and not according to how he or Sarah looked at their advanced ages. He believed according to what was spoken and not according to popular opinion. He believed according to what was spoken and not according to the doctor's report, his past history, the experiences of others, or any other thing. He believed according to what was spoken by God!

• **Abraham chose to become occupied with the promise instead of with the problem.** (Rom. 4:19,20.)

Abraham certainly was aware of both his and Sarah's physical limitations. He was aware of their past history of barrenness and of their advanced age. But rather than choosing to dwell on the problem, he chose instead to dwell on the solution. "He wavered not while looking unto the promise" (ASV). He glanced at the problem and gazed at the promise. Webster defines gaze as "to look intently or steadily."[4] Most people do just the reverse of that, and it proves to be the undoing of their faith. They glance at the promise and gaze at the problem, and by focusing on their difficulties instead of God's promised deliverance, they are robbed of their faith.

Think of Peter, who stepped out of the boat and began to walk on the water to Jesus, until he became occupied with the wind and the waves. Then he cried out for help as he began to sink. As soon as he took his focus off of Jesus and put it upon the circumstances around him, he began to sink. As Jesus caught him, He said, "O you of little faith, why did you doubt?" (Matt. 14:31). By allowing his gaze to become fixed on the storm instead of on Jesus, Peter was robbed of his faith.

Glance at the problem, but gaze at the promise and at the One who did the promising. Let yourself become occupied with our wonderful Savior, His faithfulness, and His promises. You will find your faith strengthened as you do.

• **Abraham gave glory to God in advance—he praised God for this blessing even before it happened.** (Rom. 4:20 TLB.)

The family that brought me to Christ seemed to trust God for everything. They were wonderful examples of faith. So early on, I was introduced to some of the fundamental principles of faith by simply watching them. I can still remember one afternoon when the mother, who looked deathly ill, lifted her hands and praised God for her health.

I said, "Are you okay? You don't look so good. You don't sound too good, either!" She quietly responded, "Bayless, I believe I'm healed."

I thought, *Yeah, sure!* But in just a little while, she was completely recovered. As I watched that family pray, I witnessed miraculous answers taking place, and slowly, while listening to their "praises of faith," my eyes began to open. I began to realize that there is a whole unseen realm around us, that the material world is subject to the spiritual world, and that faith is how spiritual transactions are made.

LESSONS OF FAITH FROM ELIJAH AND ELISHA

We have several distinct figures in Scripture that fulfill the role of spiritual father/mentor quite well. Two of those figures are Elijah and Elisha. Elijah served as a spiritual mentor to Elisha, teaching him the ways of God until he was caught up into heaven and Elisha cried out, "My father, my father!"

Elisha, in like manner, served as a spiritual mentor to others and was looked upon as a spiritual father. When he was about to die, Joash, the king of Israel, also cried out with the same words: "My father, my father!"

One day, while in the city of Dothan, Elisha was to give one of his sons in the Lord a lesson in faith that he would never forget. The king of Syria's troops had surrounded the city at night, specifically to apprehend Elisha. In the morning, Elisha's servant arose early only to find an alarming sight: a great army surrounding them. There was no way of escape and no way to fight—a hopeless situation. He said to Elisha, "Alas, my master! What shall we do?" So he answered, "Do not fear, for those who are with us are more than those who are with them." And Elisha prayed, and said, "Lord, I pray, open his eyes that he may see." Then the Lord opened the eyes of the young man, and he saw. And behold, the mountain was full of horses and chariots of fire all around Elisha (2 Kings 6:15-17).

Elisha had not seen the angelic troops of God or the chariots of fire any more than his servant had, but he had known they were there. He had seen them with the eyes of faith. And acting as a father in the faith, he had prayed that his servant would have the same revelation.

IMITATE THE FAITH OF GODLY FATHERS

Remember those who rule over you, who have spoken the word of God to you, whose faith follow, considering the outcome of their conduct. Jesus Christ is the same yesterday, today, and forever.

Hebrews 13:7,8

What Jesus has done for the fathers in the faith, He will do for the sons and daughters—if they will imitate the faith of their fathers.

Years ago while in Mexico, I was working with a team for several weeks, preaching in small churches and praying for the sick. One native pastor watched us closely for several days as we prayed for the sick. Suddenly, in the middle of a meeting, right when we were about to pray for a man with severe back problems, that native pastor jumped to his feet and announced, "I can do that." He proceeded to pray just as we had done, and within moments, the gentleman with the back problems was bending over and touching his toes, completely restored. I can still remember that pastor's ear-to-ear grin. It seemed to shout, "My faith will work just as the American preachers' faith will work." And he was right, because the promises of God are all yes and amen (2 Cor. 1:20) to those who will believe them by faith.

How we need spiritual fathers in the faith who will teach their sons and daughters these truths and pray that their eyes will be opened! Who will help them to understand that those who are with them are more than those who are against them? Who will show them that the truth of God's Word will change the circumstances around them if they will just dare to believe?

I have had the pleasure of knowing several great fathers in the faith, men who went out with nothing but a divine call burning in their hearts. Against impossible odds, they built great works for God. They established churches, evangelized nations, brought the gospel to places where it was previously unproclaimed (sometimes with little or no support financially from their denominations)—all because they trusted in God. Just being around men who have left a mark upon this world for good can change your life. You not only learn about faith, but their spirit of faith rubs off on you!

EXEMPLIFY WORRY-FREE, INTEGRITY-FILLED, FOCUSED LIVING

The next few steps in our spiritual fathering principles require us to live peaceful lives that are full of integrity—ever keeping our eyes on the prize. As you live these godly principles before your children, you will be a shining example of Jesus that will shape and guide their lives.

3. Be an example by living free of anxiety.

Be anxious for nothing, but in everything by prayer and supplication, with thanksgiving, let your requests be made known to God; and the peace of God, which surpasses all understanding, will guard your hearts and minds through Christ Jesus.

Finally, brethren, whatever things are true, whatever things are noble, whatever things are just, whatever things are pure, whatever things are lovely, whatever things are of good report, if there is any virtue and if there is anything praiseworthy— meditate on these things. The things which you learned and received and heard and saw in me, these do, and the God of peace will be with you.

Philippians 4:6-9

In this passage, the apostle Paul not only encouraged the Philippians to be worry-free, but he also lived that way himself. He didn't just tell them to do as he said—he told them to do as he did. Truly, his life and teaching agreed.

I was told the story about a great father in the faith who, years ago, was the president of one of Britain's oldest Pentecostal Bible schools. It seemed that the Bible school was in debt and needed a huge sum of money within days, or the owner was going to foreclose on the property. The evening before the payment was due, the board of directors and the professors of the school were in a prayer meeting. The atmosphere was gloomy. In a few hours, the doors to their great Bible college would be closed. Everyone seemed depressed except the president. There was no discernable worry on his countenance, and his prayers seemed to flow effortlessly to God. He looked over the solemn crowd and said, "Men, there is no need to worry. God has until tomorrow to get the money to us."

The others didn't seem too encouraged by his words, but still he persisted: "Don't worry. We've prayed. Now it's in God's hands."

The next morning, an unmarked package was delivered. The staff had no idea who had sent it. Upon opening it, they discovered several thousand English pound notes—just enough to pay off the Bible school's debt. What a great example of anxiety-free living!

The following testimony of a man, who committed his life to God as a boy because of watching how his father reacted in the midst of a crisis, is another great example. They were farmers in the Midwest, and even as a boy, he understood the importance that the weather played in having a successful harvest. Either too little or too much rain could prove disastrous. One year it had been unusually wet, and their entire wheat crop had been destroyed because of heavy rains. The little boy stood on the edge of the ruined field, his hand clasping the rugged and calloused hand of his father. Even though he was only ten years old, he knew what this meant: no crop, no income. Hard times were up ahead. But he was suddenly aware of something beautiful in the midst of that tragedy. His father was singing, "Rock of Ages, cleft for me…." As he looked up, he saw a tear roll down his father's face, and still the words came: "…let me hide myself in Thee."

"That day I decided to put my life in the hands of God," the boy, now a full-grown adult, testified. "I wanted to serve God like my dad, who was able to trust God and have peace even in the midst of that terrible time."

Be anxious for nothing, pray with thanksgiving, and let God's perfect peace keep your heart and mind. That's how God wants us to live today. He tells us to be anxious for nothing. We should pray, thank God, and then enjoy His peace! As fathers in the faith, we should be passing down a legacy of stress-free living to our children.

4. Be an example by keeping the heavenly prize in focus.

No, dear brothers, I am still not all I should be but I am bringing all my energies to bear on this one thing: Forgetting the past and looking forward to what lies ahead, I strain to reach the end of the race and receive the prize for which God is calling us up to heaven because of what Christ Jesus did for us. I hope all of you who are mature Christians will see eye-to-eye with me on these things, and if you disagree on some point, I believe that God will make it plain to you—if you fully obey the truth you have. Dear brothers, pattern your lives after mine, and notice who else lives up to my example. For I have told you often before, and I say it again now with tears in my eyes, there are many who walk along the Christian road who are really enemies of the cross of Christ. Their future is eternal loss, for their god is their appetite: they are proud of what they should be ashamed of; and all they think about is this life here on earth. But our homeland is in heaven, where our Savior, the Lord Jesus Christ is; and we are looking forward to his return from there.

Philippians 3:13-20 TLB

Many professing Christians today are like the people Paul wrote about in this passage of Philippians—they think only about life here on earth. But we have a responsibility to talk and live in such a way that it will cause people to say, "They must really believe in life beyond the grave. They must believe that there is a heaven and a hell and that they will be rewarded for living for Christ in this life."

Dear friend, a day of reckoning is coming, and it will be either a very positive or a very negative experience, depending on whether you served God or served yourself in this life. Every believer will stand before the judgment seat of Christ (Rom. 14:10; 2 Cor. 5:10), and every unbeliever will stand before the great white throne of judgment (Rev. 20:11-15). May we, like the apostle Paul, live our lives in anticipation of Christ's return, and may our children receive God's gracious *"Well done, thou good and faithful servant"* because they have followed our example of faith.

An elderly couple whom my wife and I know recently told us that they had made no provision for their retirement. They are in their eighties and are still working because they didn't plan for their future. They encouraged us to not be as foolish as they had been. Preparing for your future in this life is important. It is foolish not to plan when the means are available. But how much more foolish is it to not prepare for eternity?

Look at the words of Paul, speaking as a father in the faith to his spiritual son Timothy about these matters:

> **But you be watchful in all things, endure afflictions, do the work of an evangelist, fulfill your ministry. For I am already being poured out as a drink offering, and the time of my departure is at hand. I have fought the good fight, I have finished the race, I have kept the faith. Finally, there is laid up for me the crown of righteousness, which the Lord, the righteous Judge, will give to me on that Day, and not to me only but also to all who have loved His appearing.**
>
> **2 Timothy 4:5-8**

Paul was urging a young minister to fulfill his ministry even as he had fulfilled his. Why? Because of "that Day," a phrase Paul also uses in 2 Timothy 1:12 which refers to the judgment seat of Christ, where we will give an account for the lives that we as believers have lived on this earth. We will all stand together on that Day, and eternal rewards will be given—but only to those who have done the three things listed in 2 Timothy 4:7:

- Fought the good fight
- Finished the race
- Kept the faith

To those who have faithfully served the Lord in this life, a "crown" will be given. A crown represents both reward and rank. *Our position and rank in heaven will be unalterably determined by how we live for Him in this life.* Jesus taught this same truth in His parable of the talents. (Matt. 25:14-30; Luke 19:12-27.). He told of the servants who faithfully obeyed the master's wishes in his absence. Upon their master's return, they were richly rewarded—they became rulers over many things and were given authority over ten cities. On "that Day," some will be rejoicing and some will be ashamed.

When we understand the awesomeness of that Day, Paul's words in 1 Corinthians 9:24-27 make perfect sense:

> **Do you not know that those who run in a race all run, but one receives the prize? Run in such a way that you may obtain it. And everyone who competes for the prize is temperate in all things. Now they do it to obtain a perishable crown, but we for an imperishable crown. Therefore I run thus: not with uncertainty. Thus I fight: not as one who beats the air. But I discipline my body and bring it into subjection, lest, when I have preached to others, I myself should become disqualified.**

Olympic athletes do not eat all they want or work out only when they feel like it. They go through rigorous discipline for years in order to have one chance at some fleeting glory. They deny themselves legitimate pleasures and push themselves to the limits just for the chance of winning a medal that eventually will tarnish and be forgotten by following generations. When we consider the magnitude of the heavenly prize—eternal rank and reward with a crown that doesn't fade away—how much more should we be willing to discipline ourselves and serve God? We should be prepared to serve Him in season and out of season, when it is convenient and popular and when it is not, when we feel like it and when we don't. The eternal reward when we reach the end of the race and receive the prize for which God is calling us up to heaven, will be well worth our best efforts!

Writing as a spiritual father in his second epistle, John admonishes his children in the Lord: "Look to yourselves, that we do not lose those things we worked for, but that we may receive a full reward" (2 John 8). John understood that some will receive a full reward while others will lose what they have worked for and receive only a partial reward—or no reward at all!

In Revelation 22:12, Jesus said, "And behold, I am coming quickly, and My reward is with Me, to give to every one according to his work." But in Revelation 3:11, He said, "Behold, I am coming quickly! Hold fast what you have, that no one may take your crown."

The only way someone else could take your crown is to do your work! If you choose to live for yourself and not for God, the Lord has to find another person to do what He called you to do—and that person will not only do your work, but he or she will also receive your reward!

As a young man, I went to work for a university professor who owned a large country estate. He hired several young men to do manual labor, improving the landscape of the property. We spent our days removing large stones from a dry riverbed that ran through the property, trimming hedges, cutting back wild blackberry bushes, and the like. It was hard work, and he paid well. But one of my friends didn't like the work (or any kind of work, for that matter), so after we checked in each morning, he went to a remote part of the estate where a friend picked him up in a car. He stayed gone all day, returned just before quitting time, and did his best to get his hands dirty to make it look like he had worked all day.

To this day I don't know how the professor found out what was going on, but when we came at the end of the week for our pay, not only was my friend not paid—he was fired. And he should have been! It was outrageous for him to expect payment for shirking his responsibilities and letting someone else do his work.

This young man was quite embarrassed when the professor addressed him in front of us all and sent him away empty-handed. How much more embarrassing will it be on that Day for those who have not lived for God? There you and I will be in front of all the saints and martyrs who gave their lives for Christ—those who obeyed and served Him throughout the centuries—from Abraham to David to Paul to those in our generation. Angels will be looking on, but most terrifying of all, you will not be able to escape the scrutinizing gaze of the Son of God (2 Cor. 5:10,11), the One whose hair is "white like wool, as white as snow, and His eyes like a flame of fire" (Rev. 1:14), the One who was dead but is alive forevermore, who has the keys of hell and death (Rev. 1:18). What an awesome day it will be! We need to live with the heavenly prize in focus.

MOSES LOOKED TO THE REWARD

By faith Moses, when he became of age, refused to be called the son of Pharaoh's daughter, choosing rather to suffer affliction with the people of God than to enjoy the passing pleasures of sin, esteeming the reproach of Christ greater riches than the treasures in Egypt; for he looked to the reward.

Hebrews 11:24-26

When Moses made his choice, Pharaoh may have said, "You are a fool, Moses! You could have had it all—a life of ease and luxury, any woman you wanted, wealth, power, and recognition. But you chose to identify with the people of your God and to go the way of sacrifice. You are a fool!"

But Moses has received that reward he had his eye on. He is in the presence of God and has his place in God's eternal kingdom.

But what of Pharaoh? He has been burning in hell for three and a half thousand years! And his eternity only gets worse. Who was the fool?

The church needs spiritual fathers who admonish and warn those who are younger in the Lord to live for God. We need mentors who will teach our young people not to throw away their eternal rewards for a relationship with some ungodly boyfriend or girlfriend or for a handful of earthly success that will soon turn to dust!

The spiritual father's cry is this: "Live for God. Find His will. Find out what is important to Him, and do it! Live holy. Live obediently. Live generously, for we shall all stand before the judgment seat of Christ."

WHY SOME FAIL TO PRESS TOWARD THE GOAL

Some people don't press toward the goal because they are satisfied and complacent with the present. Others don't press forward because they are chained to the past. This is why Paul wrote in Philippians 3:12-14:

> **Not that I have already attained, or am already perfected; but I press on, that I may lay hold of that for which Christ Jesus has also laid hold of me. Brethren, I do not count myself to have apprehended; but one thing I do, forgetting those things which are behind and reaching forward to those things which are ahead, I press toward the goal for the prize of the upward call of God in Christ Jesus.**

Often I walk late in the evenings around our neighborhood to pray. One such evening as I was walking along enjoying my fellowship with the Lord, I came upon a very large, aggressive dog that was in someone's yard. I began to give the dog a very wide berth until I noticed that he was chained. Once I realized that, I relaxed. Even though he was barking and showing his teeth, he was no threat. He could only make noise.

Many of God's people are chained to their past failures. And as long as they continue to dwell in the past—both emotionally and mentally—tied with the chains of condemnation, they will never press toward the heavenly prize. They will never be a true threat to the devil, no matter how much noise they make! So in most cases, you need to bury your past if you want to uncover your future.

While many are chained to past failures, others are tied to past successes. I was invited to preach in a church some years ago, and to my surprise, the only ones who turned out were a handful of people from my church! The place was deserted and had the spiritual stench of a graveyard. Only the tokens of a life that once existed remained. As I spoke to the pastor who had invited me, it soon became evident that he only had one thing on his mind: a revival they had had in their church years ago. That was it—the subject dominated his conversation.

It was useless to try to discuss any other subject. He was full of glowing stories of past glory—altars that were once full of people seeking salvation and a church that was once packed to capacity. But he had no energy for the present and certainly none to press toward future goals. He was chained to a past success, which can be just as bad as being chained to a past failure.

Others, though not locked in the past, are complacent and satisfied with the present. They think they have somehow already "arrived" or "attained." They have kind of retired spiritually, feeling that they have sufficient rewards stored up.

Whether you are chained to your past or satisfied with your present, I have a word for you: *Get up!* Get up from your past failures. Get up from your past successes. Get up from your smug complacency, and press on! There are more mountains to conquer and more people to help. A heavenly prize is waiting!

We need true spiritual fathers who press toward the goal and constantly remind those in training that you never arrive! Paul provided a key: "Brethren, join in following my example, and note those who so walk, as you have us for a pattern" (Phil. 3:17).

5. Be an example by having integrity.

Spiritual fathers need to consciously and consistently serve as examples of integrity. Proverbs 20:7 says, "The righteous man walks in his integrity; his children are blessed after him." This is true of both natural and spiritual children.

Integrity has to do with honesty and uprightness, both publicly and privately. David said in Psalm 101:2, "I will walk within my house with a perfect heart [heart of integrity]." *Perfect* is the same Hebrew word translated "integrity" in Proverbs 20:7. This indicates that a righteous man walks in integrity in the privacy of his own house, where no one else can see or hear him. A person of integrity is the same privately as he or she is publicly. Spiritual fathers need to be models of integrity.

My earthly father left me the legacy of integrity, and I am grateful for it. He always told me, "Son, if you give someone your word, keep it—or die trying." He lives that way and has passed on the blueprint to me. So breaking my word is not an option. It's the same for every person of integrity.

Job said, "…Till I die I will not put away my integrity from me. My righteousness I hold fast, and will not let it go; my heart shall not reproach me as long as I live" (Job 27:5,6). To him, it was a life-and-death matter. His integrity would not allow him to agree with something that wasn't right. And that is the only way to keep a clear conscience or to keep your heart from reproaching you today.

We recently wanted to hire someone for our church staff who we felt was a perfect fit for the available position. But in the interview process, we discovered that he had a contract to work with his present employer for another nine months. So we didn't even need to pray about it. Integrity made the decision for us. For him to break his contract was to break his word. Some might say, "People break contracts like that all the time. It's common." It's true. People do—but not without breaking their integrity!

David asks the question in Psalm 15:1, "Lord, who may abide in Your tabernacle? Who may dwell in Your holy hill?" The answer, in part, is found in verse 4: "...he who swears to his own hurt and does not change." That is integrity.

I read a story recently about a preacher whose family had adopted a stray dog. Some weeks later, after hearing that his dog may have been found, the dog's owner called the family to inquire about it. After listening to the description of the dog, the owner said, "It sounds like my dog."

"How can you be sure?" the preacher asked. "Are there any special markings that would identify him? There are a lot of dogs that look like this, you know."

"Yes," the man said. "He has three coarse white hairs growing in his black tail."

The conversation ended, and the preacher examined the dog. Sure enough, there were the three white hairs. You couldn't miss them against that black tail.

Then, in the presence of his three boys, who had come to love the dog, the preacher proceeded to pull out all three white hairs. When the owner arrived to claim his dog, the preacher asked him to look for the white hairs. There were none, so the man was sent away without the dog.

Years later, as the preacher recounted the story, he said, "We kept the dog, but that day I lost three boys for Christ." They lost confidence in their father because he had not practiced what he preached.

How many young Christians have been disillusioned by the lack of integrity in the lives of those who were mentoring them in the Lord? Plenty!

We get letters all the time from people who watch our television broadcasts and were once faithful church members, but now they no longer attend because of the failings of their leaders. I don't believe it is a legitimate reason for not going to church, but it is a fact. People who have observed a lack of integrity in spiritual leadership find it hard to trust anyone.

It is important to understand that I am not talking about maintaining a standard of sinless perfection. No one qualifies there except Jesus. However, I am talking about having an honest and an upright heart. People of integrity endeavor to do what is right and to keep their word, even if it costs them.

It is a known fact that early in the history of the United States, the Quakers (Society of Friends) were extremely successful in business, partly because everyone knew they could be trusted. They had integrity, so people sought them out to do business with them. This should be true of every Christian in every generation.

Proverbs 11:3 says, "The integrity of the upright will guide them…." Once you have decided to walk in integrity, two-thirds of life's decisions are already made. If in any way it causes me to compromise my integrity, the answer is no. I don't need to think about it or pray about it, because integrity guides me.

ELEPHANT BOOTS IN AUSTRALIA

Years ago, when many stores still carried elephant-skin boots, my wife bought a pair for me. They were comfortable, and I wore them often. Later when I was preparing for a trip to preach in Australia, I packed my elephant boots without thinking twice. Upon arriving at the Sydney Airport, we were given customs forms to fill out before we could officially enter the country. I began to read down the list of contraband goods. Any firearms or other weapons? No. Any seeds or plants? No. Any leopard or elephant skins? I couldn't believe it! I checked "yes" and proceeded through the line.

The first woman to look at my passport and read my form looked as if she were going to faint. "Animal skins? What kind?" she asked in disbelief.

"Elephant-skin boots," I told her. "A gift from my wife."

"That's terrible!" she gasped. "How could you?"

"Well, they cull the elephant herds when they become too numerous, and rather than throwing away the skins, they are used to make things—like boots," I said, trying to be as disarming as I could. But she wouldn't hear any of it.

Off I was whisked to meet with a person higher up the food chain. Next I found myself being interrogated by a man who made the first woman seem docile by comparison. He rifled through my suitcase, tossing my underwear this way and my socks that way, until he held up my boots like some sort of trophy. "You Americans are terrible!" he exclaimed. "You don't care anything about the environment. We could have you turned out of the country. We should confiscate these boots and burn them." I was treated like an environmental terrorist.

Finally, after about an hour of scolding and threats, I was released—with my boots—but only after promising to take them out of the country with me when I left (as if I had planned on leaving them there). As I was gathering up my socks, underwear, and other belongings to repack everything, another employee of the airport approached me and said, "Why didn't you just say they were artificial? You could have avoided all this."

I didn't even need to think about my reply. "Because they are not artificial," I answered. "They are real. And even if they had taken my boots, it's a small price to pay compared to losing my integrity." I left the Sydney Airport that day a little ruffled but with my integrity intact.

Take someone under your wing and teach him or her through the Scriptures and by example that it is never optional for a

Christian to lie, cheat, or steal. Teach him that honesty and uprightness are Christ-like qualities that all believers should demonstrate in their lives. This is the way of a spiritual father. It will not only bring a reward to you, but it will also bring people to the Savior—because your life is the only Bible that some people will ever read. Your life is the only sermon that some people will ever hear preached. It is an awesome responsibility!

CHRISTIANITY IN WORK CLOTHES

Work is the key to success in any area of life, and your children will become excellent workers when they see your diligent work. So the fourth area we see in Scripture in which spiritual fathers need to consciously serve as examples is by having diligent work habits.

6. Be an example by having diligent work habits.

But we command you, brethren, in the name of our Lord Jesus Christ, that you withdraw from every brother who walks disorderly and not according to the tradition which he received from us. For you yourselves know how you ought to follow us, for we were not disorderly among you; nor did we eat anyone's bread free of charge, but worked with labor and toil night and day, that we might not be a burden to any of you, not because we do not have authority, but to make ourselves an example of how you should follow us. For even when we were with you, we commanded you this: If anyone will not work, neither shall he eat. For we hear that there are some who walk among you in a disorderly manner, not working at all, but are busybodies. Now those who are such we command and exhort through our Lord Jesus Christ that they work in quietness and eat their own bread.

2 Thessalonians 3:6-12

As a spiritual father, Paul served as an example of a hard worker. Though some might not readily grasp it, work is an integral part of our spiritual lives. God sees no distinction between your "church life" and your "secular life." To Him, it is one and the same. Everything you do, all the time, is a reflection of where you are in your relationship with God. It is not possible to be a truly spiritual person if you are lazy in your daily work habits.

Just as there were those in the church who were "disorderly" in Paul's day, there are "disorderly" people in church today. Sluggards, who feel as if someone else owes them a living, warm the pews every Sunday. These aren't people who can't work due to some handicap or other situation. These are "Christians" who either won't work at all or won't work very much. Scripture indicates that we should not even feed such people. The Bible goes on to call them "busybodies." They seem to have plenty of time to meddle in other people's affairs, but they can't seem to find the time to do their own work.

Paul, who was divinely called and commissioned by God to preach the gospel, said in 1 Corinthians 9:14, "Even so the Lord has commanded that those who preach the gospel should live from the gospel." In other words, ministers should receive their pay from those to whom they minister. Yet, because of the example God had called Paul to set before the Thessalonian believers, he felt he needed to set aside his right of being supported by them and set a fatherly example of diligent work and self-sufficiency.

When Paul was in Corinth, he worked with Aquila and Priscilla in the tent making trade for a year and a half while continuing his preaching. (Acts 18:1-4,11.)

In his impassioned speech to the elders of Ephesus, Paul said:

"I have coveted no one's silver or gold or apparel. Yes, you yourselves know that these hands have provided for my necessities, and for those who were with me. I have shown you in every way, by laboring like this, that you must support the weak. And

remember the words of the Lord Jesus, that He said, 'It is more blessed to give than to receive.'"

Acts 207:33-35

Even if you are called into full-time preaching ministry, there may be times (either out of necessity or because God has impressed upon you) that an example needs to be set. He may direct you to make tents—or to do some other kind of work—while maintaining your obedience to the call.

INSTALLING GLASS WHILE PREACHING THE WORD

Years ago I worked as an assistant pastor in a small town in Southern California. It was a wonderful and exciting time, and there was much to do. We not only held regular services in the church, but we also maintained weekly meetings in two neighboring towns. Because of the size of the church, they could not afford to pay me a full-time salary. But because I had just been married, there was the need of added income. So my wife worked as a nurse in a local hospital three days a week, and I took on a side job as a glass installer.

The man who employed me was a member of the church and was very gracious in allowing me flexibility in my schedule so that I could perform my church duties. Between my church salary, the money I made installing glass, and my wife's part-time income, we were able to rent a small apartment and meet all of our obligations.

After many months, I began to feel a stirring in my spirit from the Lord. He seemed to be telling me to trust Him for outside meetings and to step away from the glass work. I shared what was on my heart with my wife, Janet, and she said, "I think it is God. Do it."

Next I asked permission from the senior pastor to take outside preaching invitations if it didn't interfere with my duties in the church. To this, he gladly agreed.

I informed my boss at the glass company that I was leaving, and the rest was in God's hands. Supernaturally, invitations to preach began to pour in. Within a month, I was receiving more income from those meetings than I had been making as a glass installer. And the flow of invitations and income continued until we left to begin our own church a year later.

Someone might ask, "What if it hadn't panned out? What if no invitations to preach had come? What would you have done?" If nothing had happened within a reasonable amount of time, I would have been right back at the glass company, asking for my job back or applying for another job somewhere else—and I wouldn't have felt any less spiritual for doing so. Whether it is preaching, installing glass, or whatever we do, God wants us to be examples of diligence and hard work.

If you feel like you are called to some type of full-time ministry and the ministry is not large enough to support you, you need to have another job to supplement your income. There is no shame in that. In fact, the man who wrote almost half of the New Testament left you an example to follow.

Although working hard to supply our needs is a worthy cause, there is a higher motivation for working: blessing others.

> **"I have shown you in every way, by laboring like this, that you must support the weak. And remember the words of the Lord Jesus, that He said, 'It is more blessed to give than to receive.'"**
>
> **Acts 20:35**

The same truth is echoed in Ephesians 4:28: "Let him who stole steal no longer, but rather let him labor, working with his hands what is good, that he may have something to give him who has need."

SALVATION CHANGES EVERYTHING

I was saved out of what is referred to as "the hippie generation." Almost everyone I knew seemed to be "allergic" to work. I lived in a small college town in Oregon, and the majority of my friends, whether students or not, received free food stamps and various other support from the state and other agencies.

Though I personally never received food stamps or any of the other aid that was available, I didn't like work any more than my friends did. Along with the occasional money I received from my family, I worked at various jobs until I saved a little money, and then I quit. That was my pattern—work for a few weeks, then quit. Work, get paid, then quit. I just didn't like work!

But then I got saved! I began reading the book of Proverbs and began to find verses like these:

> **The hand of the diligent will rule, but the lazy man will be put to forced labor.**
>
> **Proverbs 12:24**

> **The soul of a lazy man desires, and has nothing; but the soul of the diligent shall be made rich.**
>
> **Proverbs 13:4**

> **He who is slothful in his work is a brother to him who is a great destroyer.**
>
> **Proverbs 18:9**

> **I went by the field of the lazy man, and by the vineyard of the man devoid of understanding; and there it was, all overgrown with thorns; its surface was covered with nettles; its stone wall was broken down. When I saw it, I considered it well; I looked on it and received instruction: A little sleep, a little slumber, a little folding of the hands to rest; so shall your poverty come like a prowler, and your need like an armed man.**
>
> **Proverbs 24:30-34**

> **Go to the ant, you sluggard! Consider her ways and be wise.**
>
> **Proverbs 6:6**

I'd spent some time observing the ants. I'd seen how hard they work, and I was definitely getting God's message loud and clear: hard work...diligence...no excuses. I immediately got a job and stayed faithful at it. I worked hard and got promoted. Work is spiritual, just as prayer is spiritual, and it needs to be done from the heart as unto the Lord.

"BUT I'M JUST A HOUSEWIFE"

"But I'm just a housewife," someone says. Don't ever say, "I'm *just* a housewife." Keeping an orderly home, cooking, cleaning, and raising children is a high calling, and it is hard work! There is also an incredible need for mentors in this area of spiritual leadership. Of older women, Paul writes that they should "...be reverent in behavior, not slanderers, not given to much wine, teachers of good things—that they admonish the young women to love their husbands, to love their children, to be discreet, chaste, homemakers, good, obedient to their own husbands, that the word of God may not be blasphemed" (Titus 2:3-5).

If you have been successful in the hard work of raising a family, loving a husband, and keeping a good home—your services are needed! There are plenty of young, Christian women who need your wisdom and example. Take someone under your wing and teach him or her what you know. In a generation where the very moral fabric of the family seems to be unraveling—with children growing up without proper guidance, the divorce rate rapidly escalating, and society preaching that there need not be any absolutes or moral standards—we desperately need women of God who will rise to the challenge of mentoring our current generation of younger women. We need women like the wife in Proverbs 31:10-31—women who will see to the physical and spiritual needs of their children, love and undergird their husbands with confidence and support, and work willingly, developing their God-given talents without losing their families. The call is sounding forth for women of God who will be mentors and examples by sharing what they have learned. Do you hear it? Will you respond?

Whether male or female, we need to be modeling a diligent work ethic. It is interesting to note that Jesus chose busy people to be His disciples—those who were fishing, or collecting taxes, and the like. He didn't round up people off the street corner who were just "passing the time." When God chose a king to replace Saul, He sent Samuel to the house of Jesse. Jesse brought his sons, one by one, before Samuel, but the Lord rejected them all. Finally, Samuel asked Jesse, "Are all your children here?"

"Well, all but one. There is the youngest, David…he's out in the field working." The one God chose to serve was the only one who was busy.

IN BOTH NATURAL AND SPIRITUAL THINGS

Even as Paul modeled responsibility and diligent work habits for those he brought to the Lord, so should we.

In spiritual matters, such as studying the Scriptures and prayer, we should be diligent to present ourselves to God as workers who don't need to be ashamed. (2 Tim. 2:15.) But we must be just as diligent in natural matters—in things as basic as showing up for work on time and putting in a full day of honest labor. In fact, I believe Christians should be such valuable and faithful employees that if they change jobs or move away, their employers hate to see them go. As employees, we should be the best combination of dependability, diligence, and good attitude that anyone has ever seen. Never forget, we are to work as unto the Lord, because someone will be watching our example!

7. Be an example by having a servant's heart.

Finally, the seventh area in which spiritual fathers need to consciously serve as examples is in the arena of servanthood. And we have no better example in Scripture of a servant than the Lord Jesus Himself. His entire life (and death) reveals a servant's heart, but we find our best portrait of the Servant-Savior in John 13 as He washes the feet of His disciples the night of His arrest.

> **Jesus, knowing that the Father had given all things into His hands, and that He had come from God and was going to God, rose from supper and laid aside His garments, took a towel and girded Himself. After that, He poured water into a basin and began to wash the disciples' feet, and to wipe them with the towel with which He was girded.**
>
> **So when He had washed their feet, taken His garments, and sat down again, He said to them, "Do you know what I have done to you? You call me Teacher and Lord, and you say well, for so I am. If I then, your Lord and Teacher, have washed your feet, you also ought to wash one another's feet. For I have given you an example, that you should do as I have done to you. Most assuredly, I say to you, a servant is not greater than his master; nor is he who is sent greater than he who sent him. If you know these things, blessed are you if you do them."**

> **John 13:3-5, 12-17**

After traveling the dusty roads of Palestine, Eastern tradition and hospitality provided a basin and water for the washing of a guest's feet upon entering any home. It was the job of the lowliest, least-esteemed servant to wash a guest's feet. So by washing the disciples' feet, Jesus displayed to any would-be spiritual father or mother the nature of true leadership in God's kingdom. We are called to humbly serve one another and to put one another first. Only then do we qualify for promotion and leadership in the body of Christ.

It is quite illuminating to see the way God chose to let this story unfold for us. It begins with an amazing revelation: *Jesus, knowing that the Father had given all things into His hands, and that He had come from God and was going to God....* Jesus knew who He was, where He came from, and where He was going. He knew His place with the Father, His authority, His deity, His rank. And because of that, He wasn't threatened to serve! Insecure people who don't know where they are in God's order of things usually want to dominate others. They are too insecure in who they are in God to serve others. You find people like this in the secular work place and in the church. Even on church staffs, you will usually find people who are always trying to "throw their weight around," making sure that everyone below them in the pecking order knows that they are in charge. It all stems from insecurity and a lack of "knowing" in their hearts that God has placed them where they are. They are unsure of their identity, and they don't understand that God will take them where they need to be if they will quietly trust Him. So, truly, having a servant's heart is predicated upon having an intimate relationship with God. Without one, you cannot have the other.

THE WAY UP IS DOWN

Then He came to Capernaum. And when He was in the house He asked them, "What was it you disputed among yourselves on the road?" But they kept silent, for on the road they had disputed among themselves who would be the greatest. And He sat down, called the twelve, and said to them, "If anyone desires to be first, he shall be last of all and servant of all."

Mark 9:33-35

That must have been one interesting conversation on the road! You would think that once Jesus had made their error clear, this issue of "who would be greatest" wouldn't come up again. But, alas, just a few verses later they are at it again:

Then James and John, the sons of Zebedee, came to Him, saying, "Teacher, we want You to do for us whatever we ask." And He said to them, "What do you want Me to do for you?" They said to Him, "Grant us that we may sit, one on Your right hand and the other on Your left, in Your glory." But Jesus said to them, "You do not know what you ask. Are you able to drink the cup that I drink, and be baptized with the baptism that I am baptized with?" And they said to Him, "We are able." So Jesus said to them, "You will indeed drink the cup that I drink, and with the baptism I am baptized with you will be baptized; but to sit on My right hand and on My left is not Mine to give, but it is for those for whom it is prepared." And when the ten heard it,

they began to be greatly displeased with James and John. But Jesus called them to Himself and said to them, "You know that those who are considered rulers over the Gentiles lord it over them, and their great ones exercise authority over them. Yet it shall not be so among you; but whoever desires to become great among you shall be your servant. And whoever of you desires to be first shall be slave of all. For even the Son of Man did not come to be served, but to serve, and to give His life a ransom for many."

Mark 10:35-45

It's clear—the way up is down, and the first shall be last. The leader shall be servant of all. But oh, how slowly our hearts warm to this truth! Even as the disciples seemed incapable at first of grasping it, we also find it difficult to comprehend—and even more difficult to implement.

To the natural mind, assuming the role of a servant connotes weakness or a lack of moral fiber and decision-making ability. But the reality is that only a strong, assured leader can take on the voluntary role of a servant without hesitation. True spiritual leaders know that they are not somehow stripped of their authority or robbed of their ability to lead when they stoop to wash feet. On the contrary, their authority is confirmed by God.

Good leaders and spiritual fathers know that they must sometimes make hard decisions and exercise their authority, even when others may not agree. But they also know that if they have modeled a servant's heart to those they presume to lead, their followers will be willing to follow them through the tough times. Servants demonstrate their ability to lead by showing that they care.

True spiritual leaders never grow out of servanthood, no matter how successful they become. In my traveling, I have been privileged to meet and preach for some wonderful pastors who, in some cases, preside over congregations of thousands.

One such pastor, who is without a doubt one of the most influential ministers in his nation, demonstrated his own need for some re-education in the area of servanthood. I happened to be sitting near him during a meeting in his church, where more than seven thousand people attend each Sunday. I noticed a small piece of paper lying near his feet. When the pastor saw the paper, he motioned for one of his elders (who was about twenty feet away) to come over and to pick it up. He either felt he was too important to pick up a gum wrapper or he wanted to exercise his authority by ordering a subordinate to do what he could have done himself. Either way, his actions demonstrated the heart of a master and not the heart of a servant.

By contrast, I was preaching recently for the pastor of the largest Protestant church in his nation. This man was also the most well-known minister in that nation. As I was driving one afternoon with one of his assistant pastors, he related to me the history of the magnificent tabernacle they had built to house the ever-growing congregation. "Bayless," he said, "there were days that we literally had to chase the pastor off the building site. He would be out there pounding nails with the rest of the workers, many of whom were volunteers from the church, and he wouldn't want to leave. 'Pastor, go home and study,' we would say. But he would respond by simply telling us that he wanted to be with us."

Undoubtedly, the pastor should have been tending to more important matters, but his attitude of heart is to be commended. Though a strong leader and a marvelous preacher, he had not forgotten the words of Jesus: "Whoever desires to be great among you shall be your servant."

SERVE THE LORD AND SERVE OTHERS

"We are called first to serve the Lord: Serve the Lord with gladness…" (Ps. 100:2). Second, we are called to serve one another: "…through love serve one another" (Gal. 5:13). Third, we are called to serve those outside of the church by meeting practical needs and by bringing them the gospel: "…I have made myself a servant to all..." (1 Cor. 9:19). Whichever of the categories we might be serving in, it basically means that I am putting someone else before myself in both my thinking and my lifestyle, whether it be family, friends, strangers, or God.

FIVE THINGS ARE REQUIRED IN ORDER TO SERVE GOD

To be a servant of the Lord, five things are required:

1. **A listening ear—to both His Word and His Spirit in order to find out His will. (Isa. 30:21; Mark 4:24.)**

2. **Obedience—in order to carry out His will once we know it. (1 Peter 1:13-15.)**

3. **Faithfulness—to stay at it when things aren't easy or don't go our way. (Matt. 25:21; Gal. 5:22.)**

4. **Loyalty—for no man can serve two masters. (Matt. 6:24.)**

5. **Gentleness— a servant of the Lord must not quarrel but be gentle to all. (2 Tim. 2:24.)**

SERVING OTHERS

To be a servant to others, whether in or outside of the church, you need to understand the value of a person. God paid the ultimate price for all people with the life and blood of His Son. That's value! When this truth begins to dawn upon you, it suddenly becomes reasonable to pour your life out for other people.

It also helps to realize that there is a reward for servanthood. God exalts those who humble themselves. Elisha, after faithfully serving Elijah, got a double portion of his spirit. Gehazi, who was chosen as the successor of Elisha, got nothing—except leprosy— because, unlike Elisha his predecessor, Gehazi was more interested in being served than in serving. He lied to Naaman the Syrian to obtain monies that Elisha had refused, and later the prophet exposed him. The motives of his heart were laid bare when Elisha asked him, "Is it time to receive money and to receive clothing, olive groves and vineyards, sheep and oxen, male and female servants?" Gehazi wanted "the good life." He wanted to be master, not a servant, and he was willing to deceive in order to achieve his goal. But his only reward was the leprosy of Naaman that would cling to him and his descendants forever. (2 Kings 5:20-27.)

PRACTICING WHAT THEY PREACH

We have some dear friends in Missouri, Jeff and Patsy Perry, who pastor St. Louis Family Church, located in the beautiful Chesterfield Valley. The valley was protected from flooding by a large agricultural levy, which no one ever dreamed would break. But on the last day of July 1993, at 8:00 A.M. on Friday morning, the unthinkable happened. Pastor Perry received a phone call from a member of the local Chamber of Commerce informing him that the levy was in danger of bursting and that a "volunteer evacuation" was in progress.

The Perrys and their congregation had worked for a solid year to get into their new facility (a rented warehouse that they had spent $300,000 converting into a beautiful church). The pastor and a crew from the church worked feverishly and managed to empty the building—chairs, computers, equipment, and all. They did it in three hours, putting everything into a rented space on higher ground. While they worked, several businessmen from the surrounding buildings stood by and smoked their cigarettes, mocking and laughing at the absurdity of anyone thinking there might actually be a flood.

But at 10:00 P.M. that same night, all the laughing stopped as millions of gallons of water began pouring into the valley through the just-broken levy. One billion dollars' worth of damage occurred in one day! Businesses were lost, homes were ruined, and the

St. Louis Family Church building had ten feet of mud, water, tree branches, frogs, and poisonous snakes in it!

It was devastating, but God spoke to Pastor Perry's heart, telling him to use the opportunity to be a servant to the community. So he immediately went to the mayor and volunteered his people to help clean up the devastation in the community. Instead of concentrating on rebuilding their church, the congregation determined to put their neighbors first.

In a meeting with several key city leaders a few days later, Pastor Perry announced that they were going to pray and begin to clean up businesses. His statement was met with a fair bit of skepticism, but when the water subsided two-and-a-half weeks later, the members of St. Louis Family Church went to work. Nearly three hundred people began serving the community through their clean-up efforts. They fed people, arranged for vaccinations by church-member doctors, and in very practical ways, began loving people and showing them Christianity in terms they could understand. Volunteers began to pour in from all over the U.S. and Canada—eight thousand in all—and they were directed and overseen by the church.

The community was dumbfounded. Here was a group of Christians, working for free—rebuilding homes, cleaning up local businesses and feeding people—while their own church remained unusable. In fact, it took an entire year for their church to be repaired, during which time the congregation met in a local Presbyterian church and a Catholic high school. It was the first time that many of the local people had ever seen Christianity in work clothes, and it got their attention.

The whole church was voted "Citizens of the Year," and the mayor broke down and wept as he presented the award. News spread and the church began to grow because people wanted to attend the church that practiced what it preached. National attention was given to Pastor Perry and his congregation.

Today the Perrys' church is several thousand strong and growing rapidly. They also have a highly effective branch of ministry that provides disaster relief around the world. God has elevated them to a position of influence in their city, across their nation, and into the world because they took on the role of a servant.

JESUS IS OUR SUPREME EXAMPLE

When it comes to humility and true servanthood, we have no greater example than the Lord Jesus Christ himself. Because Jesus humbled himself and took on the form of a servant, God exalted Him higher than any other. And we are encouraged to adopt the same attitude:

> **Let this mind be in you which was also in Christ Jesus, who, being in the form of God, did not consider it robbery to be equal with God, but made Himself of no reputation, taking the form of a bond servant, and coming in the likeness of men. And being found in appearance as a man, He humbled Himself and became obedient to the point of death, even the death of the cross. Therefore God also has highly exalted Him and given Him the name which is above every name, that at the name of Jesus every knee should bow, of those in heaven, and of those on earth, and of those under the earth, and that every tongue should confess that Jesus Christ is Lord, to the glory of God the Father.**
>
> **Philippians 2:5-11**

As we make the commitment to walk as living examples, our lives must exhibit diligent work habits and godly servanthood. As spiritual fathers, it is imperative that we model a servant's heart to those who look to us for guidance in the Lord. Our heart will be reproduced in those who follow us. Having taken up the mantle of a servant, we will be able to say, along with the apostle Paul, "Imitate me, just as I also imitate Christ" (1 Cor. 11:1).

TRUE FATHERS IN THE LORD EXHORT, COMFORT, AND CHARGE

> I do not write these things to shame you, but as my beloved children I warn you. For though you might have ten thousand instructors in Christ, yet you do not have many fathers; for in Christ Jesus I have begotten you through the gospel. Therefore I urge you, imitate me. For this reason I have sent Timothy to you, who is my beloved and faithful son in the Lord, who will remind you of my ways in Christ, as I teach everywhere in every church.
>
> **1 Corinthians 4:14-17**

As a father in the Lord, Paul modeled the Christian life, which is, by far, the most powerful tool in the arsenal of spiritual mentoring. But along with living it before them, he also "warned" (v. 14) and "taught" (v. 17) them. We find similar statements in 1 Thessalonians, where Paul was addressing another group of "children in the Lord." In this passage, perhaps more than anywhere else in Scripture, the heart of a spiritual father is revealed:

> But we were gentle among you, just as a nursing mother cherishes her own children. So, affectionately longing for you, we were well pleased to impart to you not only the gospel of God, but also our own lives, because you had become dear to us. For you

remember, brethren, our labor and toil; for laboring night and day, that we might not be a burden to any of you, we preached to you the gospel of God. You are witnesses, and God also, how devoutly and justly and blamelessly we behaved ourselves among you who believe; as you know how we exhorted, and comforted, and charged every one of you, as a father does his own children, that you would have a walk worthy of God who calls you into His own kingdom and glory.

1 Thessalonians 2:7-12

The first thing that is unmistakable in these words is the tender love that a "father in the faith" has for his children. Have you ever seen how gently a new mother cares for her nursing babe? That was Paul's heart toward the Thessalonians. He "cherished" and "affectionately longed" for them. They were "dear" to him. This is the language of love spoken by a father who felt the heavenly constraint of overseeing their souls. Paul did more than simply impart information to them. He imparted his very life, which can't be done without both time and energy. He spent much of that time and energy doing three things: *exhorting, comforting,* and *charging.* In fact, I interpret the original text to say that Paul exhorted and comforted and charged each one of them, individually, one by one. Generally, spiritual mentoring is done "one-on-one." It can happen in a group setting, but the real issues of character and maturity are tackled individually.

Individual, heart-to-heart communication is the key to reproducing in another what God has produced in you. For this reason, I try to take every opportunity to get alone with key staff members at our church. I have come to realize that the most effective impartation of what I have and who I am takes place on an individual level.

Every true father in the Lord *exhorts, comforts,* and *charges* those entrusted to his care to walk worthy of God. As we explore what each of these terms means, it will help enrich your understanding of the spiritual father's role. I will present the list in reverse order.

CHARGING SPIRITUAL CHILDREN

…We…charged every one of you, as a father does his own children.

1 Thessalonians 2:11

According to *Strong's Concordnace,* the word *charge* means "to testify or take to record."[1] It comes from the root word translated "witnesses" in 1 Thessalonians 2:10—a father testifies as a witness to his children. But you can't be a witness and testify about something you don't know, haven't experienced, or haven't seen.

If a major traffic accident occurred at a nearby corner, injuring several people, you couldn't serve as a witness to the accident unless you had been there. To try to do so without having observed the accident would be ridiculous. Even though you "heard about" the accident, your testimony would be useless in establishing any facts because you were not there. You can only be a witness to what you know and to what you have experienced.

Spiritual fathers serve as witnesses because they know something! They testify to what they have experienced, and their testimony carries much weight. They have tasted and seen that the Lord is good. They have experienced miraculous answers to prayer. They have seen God's faithfulness, mercy, and justice in action.

I have testified countless times that God delivers from drugs and alcohol. I know this is true because He did it for me. One time as I was sharing a portion of my testimony in a Sunday service, I felt especially compelled to give some details as to how I was set free from alcoholism. Prior to coming to Christ, I had "major league" problems with both drugs and alcohol. For years I had used about every kind of drug imaginable, and I was worse when it came to alcohol.

That all changed the evening I opened my heart to Christ. That night was the last time I have had a drug in my body. I was instantly delivered! (At this writing, it has been twenty-five years! Thank God for His wonderful grace!)

With alcohol, it was different. My problems with alcohol started when I was a young teenager. By the time I was an adult, I was drinking every day. I found it hard to function without being intoxicated—many times I was drunk by ten or eleven o'clock in the morning. For about two weeks after I was saved, I still continued to drink. But something was working in me, and I knew it. It was the life of God. The day after my conversion, I was sharing my testimony of how Jesus had delivered me from drugs with a close friend. He stopped me in mid-sentence and said, "I don't doubt that you have had some kind of experience and gone through a change—and maybe you won't use drugs anymore—but I know you too well, Bayless. You will never stop drinking."

Not yet having my mind renewed to God's way of thinking, I had to agree with my friend. "Something has happened to me," I said. "But you're probably right."

We were both wrong though, because over the next fourteen days, something amazing began to happen to me. I began to lose my taste for alcohol. I still remember sitting on a park bench behind a local import store where I used to buy foreign beer. I had bought a six-pack, and as I sat there finishing a couple of beers, I said to myself, "I don't need this anymore." I threw the remaining four bottles of beer in the trash. I also poured a bottle of wine down the toilet when I got home—and from that day, I have been free from alcohol.

A few weeks after sharing that story, I was approached by a man in our congregation who works in the entertainment industry. Because of the nature of his particular job, he is constantly surrounded by alcohol. For about fifteen years, he had struggled with drinking, even though he was a Christian. But that day as I testified, something happened in his heart. He told me, "As you were sharing how you stopped drinking, something said to me, 'If he did it, so can you.'"

And he did—he quit! It has been years since he has had any alcohol!

If God has done something for you—if you have personally experienced it—you can be a witness. You can testify of His goodness. There are people in our churches who have been set free by the power of God from every imaginable evil, and they need to lift their voices and tell their stories. There are always other people who desperately need to hear what they have to say.

It reminds me of a middle-aged man who served in a key leadership role in our church. He was delivered from twenty-five years of homosexuality! He became a powerful witness that Christ can deliver people from deviate sexual behavior. I am also reminded of another member of our church who was saved out of twenty-five years of heroin addiction. He has been free for five years now and has a powerful testimony! Another man I've had the privilege of serving was saved, filled with the Spirit, and delivered from twenty-eight years of alcoholism on a beautiful Easter morning about ten years ago. He is now a bold witness. And there are countless others who have been delivered from fear, healed of diseases, and had their marriages restored. Others have been lifted from despair and set free from hopelessness. What has God done for you? What do you know for sure, by experience? Tell somebody! Encourage them in the Lord!

> **We have heard with our ears, O God, our fathers have told us, the deeds You did in their days, in days of old: You drove out the nations with Your hand, but them You planted; You afflicted the peoples, and cast them out. For they did not gain possession of the land by their own sword, nor did their own arm save them; but it was Your right hand, Your arm, and the light of Your countenance, because You favored them. You are my King, O God; command victories for Jacob. Through You we will push down our enemies; through Your name we will trample those who rise up against us. For I will not trust in my bow, nor shall my sword**

save me. But You have saved us from our enemies, and have put to shame those who hated us. In God we boast all day long, and praise Your name forever. Selah.

Psalm 44:1-8

If our children are to put their trust in the Lord instead of in their "bow and sword" and if they are to make their boast in God, the fathers must first do their job of proclaiming the works and favor of God in their day.

I was talking to a minister friend recently who was really "down." A trusted staff member had just betrayed him, and it was causing some difficulties in his church. It just happened that sometime before that, I had spent several days with another friend who had experienced the same type of problem in his church, only far worse. A relative on his staff had led a mutiny and caused not only a church split but also brought much personal pain and anguish to my friend. While the wounds were still fresh and the problem still loomed large on the landscape of his future, I observed something wonderful. This pastor never said an unkind word about the one who had caused all the problems. He remained silent even when he was being publicly denounced from the pulpit by his Absalom-spirited relative who had taken several hundred of his flock and started a new church.

My friend had been lied about and betrayed, but he acted like a prince. When he was being cursed, he blessed. Instead of returning evil for evil, he prayed for his persecutors. He retaliated by blessing them and committing the situation to God. (Matt. 5:43-48; 1 Peter 2:20-23; 3:8,9.) And God vindicated him and added to the church, numerically and financially. And today they are in a much stronger position than ever.

I can testify about this situation because I watched it happen. So when I told my discouraged minister friend about that incident, it was just what he needed to hear. I could sense his spirit lift, even as we talked.

> I will open my mouth in a parable; I will utter dark sayings of old, which we have heard and known, and our fathers have told us. We will not hide them from their children, telling to the generation to come the praises of the Lord, and His strength and His wonderful works that He has done. For He established a testimony in Jacob, and appointed a law in Israel, which He commanded our fathers, that they should make them known to their children; that the generation to come might know them, the children who would be born, that they may arise and declare them to their children, that they may set their hope in God, and not forget the works of God, but keep His commandments.

Psalm 78:2-7

God commanded Israel's fathers, by divine law, to tell each new generation of the praises, strength, and wonderful works of the Lord. It was a practice that was to perpetuate itself from generation to generation. Every new generation of fathers was to testify to their children, who, in turn, were to testify to their children. The end result would be that the children would set their hope in God and obey His commands. Is this practice any less necessary today in our dispensation? The answer is obvious. We must charge those in the church today as a father does his own children.

COMFORTING SPIRITUAL CHILDREN

> We...comforted...every one of you, as a father does his own children.

1 Thessalonians 2:11

The word *comfort* in this verse means "encourage, to console."[2] I would add to that definition, "to strengthen or cheer, to speak soothingly to." It is the same word used when the Jews came to comfort Mary and Martha about the death of their brother Lazarus. (John 11:19.)

All of us go through difficult times, and we all need comforting at different seasons in our life. Fathers in the faith are especially sensitive to those who are suffering, down, or discouraged. They go out of their way to lift and comfort people.

Some time ago, the son of a woman in our church attempted suicide and failed—but just barely. He had consumed a vast number of prescription drugs, and when he was found, he had been in a coma for some time. The doctors held out no hope for his survival and said that even if he didn't die, he would be nothing more than a vegetable because the drugs had been in his body too long. His brain was destroyed. It was a devastating situation by any measure.

Imagine the sorrow and pain of his mother as she helplessly watched her son in that hopeless condition. Fortunately, this story has a good ending. A couple in our church took it upon themselves to comfort this mother and pray for her son. For several weeks, they visited her and her son, praying over his motionless body, which was hooked up to all kinds of tubes and monitors in the hospital. Then the amazing happened: the young man woke up, and his mind was fully intact. A few days later, he walked down the aisle of our church and rededicated his life to Christ. Today he is in ministry training! Thank God for comforters and for the grace of God!

In 1 Thessalonians 5:14, we are told to "…comfort the fainthearted." Do you know people who are fainthearted—ready to cave in spiritually or emotionally? If you do—and probably all of us do—call them, write them a letter, take them to lunch! Find a way to comfort them with the same comfort that you have experienced in God. Paul understood this, and so can you.

> **Blessed be the God and Father of our Lord Jesus Christ, the Father of mercies and God of all comfort, who comforts us in all our tribulation, that we may be able to comfort those who are in any trouble, with the comfort with which we ourselves are comforted by God.**
>
> **2 Corinthians 1:3,4**

EXHORTING SPIRITUAL CHILDREN

We exhorted...every one of you, as a father does his own children.

1 Thessalonians 2:11

I define the word *exhortation* as a message of warning or encouragement designed to motivate people to action. Exhortation is a two-edged sword. To exhort someone is to give them a spiritual pep talk. So the first aspect of exhortation is encouragement. The exhorter is like the basketball coach who calls a time-out when he sees the momentum shift to the opposing team. He senses that his players are feeling overwhelmed. So he gets them over to the side-lines and says something like this: "Settle down and just play your game. You can beat these guys. You are better than they are. Don't let them get you out of your game. Slow things down, play smart, and take high percentage shots, and I guarantee we'll win!" By the time the coach is done, his boys are ready to go back out and play again—only now they see victory and not defeat.

In the same way, when you sense that your brothers or sisters are struggling and it seems as if the momentum has shifted to the enemy, pull them aside and exhort them. Remind them that Jesus has already won the war and that the devil is defeated. Encourage them to stay steady, trust God, and keep praising, assuring them that God will bring them through.

Barnabas possessed this gift of encouragement. In fact, at one time his name was Joses. (Acts 4:36.) But because of his ability to encourage people, the apostles apparently renamed him Barnabas. I have read that his name meant "Son of Encouragement." There are several places in Scripture that give us glimpses of this exhorter in action. In Acts 11:23 we read of him encouraging the saints at Antioch to continue in the Lord. In Acts 14:22 we find him strengthening the souls of the disciples and exhorting them to continue in the faith.

Oh, that we had an army of people with the "Barnabas heart"! We need an army of encouragers and soul-strengtheners who have decided to take the responsibility of growing up spiritually—people who have made the determination not to always be the needy ones themselves, but to represent God as messengers of encouragement, extending His hand of blessing to those in need.

The other side of the principle of exhortation has to do with warning. This is the type of encouragement that takes place when you urge someone to walk "the straight and narrow" to avoid future consequences. The word is used in this manner in Luke 3:16-18, where John the Baptist warned the Jews that the Messiah would come with winnowing fan in hand, separating the wheat from the chaff. It is a clear warning concerning the outcome of those who only dress in the garments of religion but deny its heart. Verse 18 says, "And with many other exhortations he preached to the people."

An integral part of being a spiritual father is warning and correcting children. Remember, Paul said, "...as my beloved children I warn you" (1 Cor. 4:14). This same principle is echoed in Proverbs 3:11-12. Solomon writes, "My son, do not despise the chastening of the Lord, nor detest His correction; for whom the Lord loves He corrects, just as a father the son in whom he delights."

I can remember when I was a brand-new babe in Christ, enjoying fellowship at the home of a lady who went to our church. We were about to have some ice cream when several of the people there became engrossed in conversation about some passage from the Bible. The ice cream was temporarily put on hold when one of the ladies suggested that we all "wait on the Lord." Because I had been born again for only a few days, I didn't have a clue what that meant. I watched them as they closed their eyes and became quiet.

Then I did the only thing I knew how to do that even slightly resembled what they were doing. I closed my eyes and assumed an attitude of meditation. But it wasn't biblical meditation—it was something I had learned while studying kundalini yoga before I was saved. As I began to open up my mind to the spirit world, as I had done so many times before I received Christ, the owner of the house warned, "Bayless, what are you doing? Stop it! That's not of God! You are opening yourself to the wrong kind of spirits! Don't ever do that in my house again!"

"Okay," I said. "I didn't know. Thank you." It shocked me, but I was glad for the exhortation! I had somebody looking out for my soul, and somehow there was a great sense of security in it. However, I must say, when we were done, I ate my ice cream with fear and trembling!

HOW DO YOU WARN AND CORRECT SOMEONE?

The fact that spiritual mentors must warn and correct people stands granite solid. But how we warn and correct those people is equally as important. We should never break a person's spirit or try to shame anyone into obedience. (1 Cor. 4:14.) There is a better way. Look at how Paul opens his first letter to the Corinthian Christians:

> **I thank my God always concerning you for the grace of God which was given to you by Christ Jesus, that you were enriched in everything by Him in all utterance and all knowledge, even as the testimony of Christ was confirmed in you, so that you come short in no gift, eagerly waiting for the revelation of our Lord Jesus Christ.**

> **1 Corinthians 1:4-7**

He begins by affirming them: "You have been given grace by God. You are enriched in everything, in utterance and knowledge. You come behind in no gift. You have something very genuine going on, and God is with you." But then look at what he says next:

> **Now I plead with you, brethren, by the name of our Lord Jesus Christ, that you all speak the same thing, and that there be no divisions among you, but that you be perfectly joined together in the same mind and in the same judgment. For it has been declared to me concerning you, my brethren, by those of Chloe's household, that there are contentions among you. Now I say this,**

that each of you says, "I am of Paul," or "I am of Apollos" or "I am of Cephas," or "I am of Christ." Is Christ divided? Was Paul crucified for you? Or were you baptized in the name of Paul?

1 Corinthians 1:10-13

And I, brethren, could not speak to you as to spiritual people but as to carnal, as to babes in Christ. I fed you with milk and not with solid food; for until now you were not able to receive it, and even now you are still not able; for you are still carnal. For where there are envy, strife, and divisions among you, are you not carnal and behaving like mere men? For when one says, "I am of Paul," and another, "I am of Apollos," are you not carnal?

1 Corinthians 3:1-4

Paul corrected the Corinthians for allowing division in their midst. He said they were carnal and could not be spoken to as spiritual people. He exhorted them by acknowledging that they were acting like the unsaved with all the envy, strife, and division in their midst. Ouch! No doubt, his words cut them to the heart, but he didn't start with his correction. He began by praising them, to soften the blow. He began by pointing out what they were doing right before he pointed out what they were doing wrong. His affirmation paved the way for his rebuke and enabled them to accept it.

Too many in the body of Christ just "lay into people," telling them all that they are doing wrong and everywhere they are falling short, without one word to build them up.

The result? People with crushed spirits or people who reject the correction altogether. So please remember, when you correct and warn people—even if you feel urgently pressed—it would be worth your while (and theirs) to first think of some points you can praise them on before "just letting them have it."

JESUS IS THE MASTER

The Lord Jesus Himself is the Master at dealing with those in need of the exhortation of correction. May we take His method to heart as we deal with those under our care. We see His loving yet firm approach in John 21:

> After these things Jesus showed Himself again to the disciples at the Sea of Tiberias, and in this way He showed Himself: Simon Peter, Thomas called the Twin, Nathanael of Cana in Galilee, the sons of Zebedee, and two others of His disciples were together. Simon Peter said to them, "I am going fishing." They said to him, "We are going with you also." They went out and immediately got into the boat, and that night they caught nothing. But when the morning had now come, Jesus stood on the shore; yet the disciples did not know that it was Jesus. Then Jesus said to them, "Children, have you any food?" They answered Him, "No." And He said to them, "Cast the net on the right side of the boat, and you will find some." So they cast, and now they were not able to draw it in because of the multitude of fish. Therefore that disciple whom Jesus loved said to Peter, "It is the Lord!" Now when Simon Peter heard that it was the Lord, he put on his outer garment (for he had removed it), and plunged into the sea. But the other disciples came in the little boat (for they were not far from land, but about two hundred cubits), dragging the net with fish. Then, as soon as they had come to land, they saw a fire of coals there, and fish laid on it, and bread. Jesus said to them, "Bring some of the fish which you have just caught." Simon Peter went up and dragged the net to land, full of large fish, one hundred and fifty-three; and although there were so many, the net was not broken. Jesus said to them, "Come and eat breakfast." Yet none of the disciples dared ask Him, "Who are You?"—knowing that it was the Lord. Jesus then came and took the bread and gave it to them, and likewise the fish. This is now the third time Jesus showed Himself to His disciples after He was raised from the dead.
>
> John 21:1-14

A casual reading of this passage will overlook some of the great truths that are buried here. There is far more than meets the eye, if one is willing to dig a little bit.

First of all, Peter and the disciples were in Galilee at the Lord's bidding. Prior to the Lord's arrest and crucifixion, He had told them, "After I have been raised, I will go before you to Galilee" (Matt. 26:32). That message was confirmed again as an angel told several women after the resurrection, "And go quickly and tell His disciples that He is risen from the dead, and indeed He is going before you into Galilee; there you will see Him…" (Matt. 28:7). And if that wasn't enough already, as the women were hurrying to bring the news to the disciples, Jesus met them and said, "…Go and tell my brethren to go to Galilee, and there they will see Me" (Matt. 28:10).

The disciples were Galileans who were in Jerusalem with Jesus for the Passover feast. So no doubt, they looked forward to returning home. Following His resurrection, the Lord had appeared to them twice, and now they were on their way to meet Him in Galilee. It's not too hard to imagine what the trip home was like. Their initial shock and horror was now replaced by an air of expectancy. Not only would they be with family and friends again, but also thoughts of resuming their former fellowship with Jesus were exhilarating. I can see them talking and laughing as they traveled along the road together, occasionally breaking out into a song of praise. When they arrived in Galilee, there was no sign of Jesus. One day rolled into the next, and still He did not appear. Before long, I expect their laughter turned into sorrow and their singing into discouragement, because waiting for the Lord can, at times, be the most difficult task of all.

Hadn't Jesus said He would meet them in Galilee? Where was He? Was it all a dream? How long must they wait?

Finally, the wait became too much, and Peter blurted out, "I am going fishing." In the original text, Peter's statement is in the continuous verb form. So he wasn't just going out to catch dinner. He literally said, "I'm going fishing, and I'm going to continue fishing. I'm going back to fishing as a way of life." The other disciples said, "We're going with you, also."

You see, when Peter and the others left their boats and nets to follow Jesus, they did just that. They left them. But they didn't burn them, as Elisha had done with his plowing instruments when he'd followed Elijah. So when they returned to Galilee, everything was still there: the boats, the nets, and all their gear. As they waited for some sign of Jesus, Peter began to contemplate his old life. He saw his boats and nets. The smell of the lake filled his nostrils. Thoughts of hauling in the nets full of fish under the starry Galilean night flooded his mind. And that's when he made his decision, which is hard to fathom.

Peter had lived and ministered with Jesus and the others for over three years. He'd witnessed Jesus' miracles and had been used himself to heal the sick. He had denied the Lord once, but afterwards, found forgiveness. And now, after seeing Jesus twice after His resurrection, and receiving a commission to carry on the work of preaching the gospel, he says, "I'm going back to fishing!" He was abandoning the call! He was turning his back on the ministry, and the others followed.

That night they caught nothing (because there is nothing for you outside of the will of God!). They tried every spot they knew on the lake but couldn't catch a single fish. Rowing from place to place, they would drop the nets—but instead of their nets filling with fish, their minds filled with dark thoughts of failure and discouragement. What a depressing sight they must have been— but there was Someone watching them. Jesus knew exactly where they were and what they had done. He had gone before them into

Galilee, and He was watching them even though He had chosen not to reveal Himself to them yet.

In the morning, Jesus appeared on the shore and called out, "Have you caught any fish?" Their answer didn't surprise Him at all, because He was surely the One responsible for their empty nets. I am convinced that the risen, omnipotent Lord sent out some kind of signal to the fish in the lake that day to stay clear of one particular boat. Then after He told the disciples to cast the net on the right side of the boat, 153 of the largest fish that had obeyed His command to swim away responded to His new command to swim into the net. The disciples recognized it was the Lord, and when they got to shore with their catch of fish, they found breakfast waiting.

Jesus knew these men needed to be dealt with. He knew they needed to be rebuked and corrected for their impatience and unfaithfulness. But He also knew they were tired, hungry, and discouraged. So before He corrected them, He put some spirit back into them. He let them get dry and warm by the fire before feeding and serving them—then He let them have it!

So when they had eaten breakfast, Jesus said to Simon Peter, "Simon, son of Jonah, do you love Me more than these?" (v. 15). Jesus wasn't pointing to the disciples when he asked Peter that question. He was pointing to a boat, some nets, and 153 fish flopping on the shore: "Do you love me more than these?" If you do, feed My lambs and feed My sheep! You aren't called to catch fish, Peter. You are called to minister to people!" (John 21:15-17.) Peter and the other "children" were corrected and restored by Jesus. And, in so doing, Jesus left a pattern for every spiritual father to follow in correcting his children.

Someone in your spiritual care may need to be rebuked, warned, or corrected. But it is hard to receive a rebuke or be corrected when you are tired, wet, cold, hungry, and discouraged. So take the cue from Jesus. Before "lowering the boom" on someone, fix him a sandwich and a cup of tea. Try to lift his spirit a bit, and then correct him. You will have far better results than if you just "lay into him."

Every father in the faith will need to testify to, comfort, and exhort his spiritual children. If you know someone right now who has drifted from his "first love" and is discouraged or battling with temptation, why not minister to him? God will help you. He will give you the words and the way to reach him. Trust Him to guide you. It's no coincidence that you are reading this right now. God may want to use you to help one of His children.

THREE CATEGORIES OF PEOPLE

> **But this is what was spoken by the prophet Joel: "'And it shall come to pass in the last days, says God, that I will pour out of My Spirit on all flesh; your sons and your daughters shall prophesy, your young men shall see visions, your old men shall dream dreams.'"**

> **Acts 2:16,17**

When Peter quoted from the prophet Joel in this passage to explain the infilling of the Spirit experienced by the disciples on Pentecost, three distinct classes of people were mentioned. First, sons and daughters (or children); second, young men; and third, old men (or fathers). All three classes of people are affected by the Spirit's outpouring in the last days. Though all three designations can refer to natural age groups, they can also refer to people in different stages of spiritual growth.

John refers to the same three categories of spiritual development in his first epistle:

> **I write to you, little children, because your sins are forgiven you for His name's sake. I write to you, fathers, because you have known Him who is from the beginning. I write to you, young men,**

because you have overcome the wicked one. I write to you, little children, because you have known the Father. I have written to you, fathers, because you have known Him who is from the beginning. I have written to you, young men, because you are strong, and the word of God abides in you, and you have overcome the wicked one.

1 John 2:12-14

It is interesting to note that John uses two different Greek words here for little children: *teknion* and *paidion*. These words together describe the human ages that fall between infancy and about twelve years old, showing us that spiritual childhood covers quite a wide range of people. Next are the young men—those who are more knowledgeable and mature in the Lord. And, finally, Peter spoke of the fathers, the "old men" who have reached spiritual adulthood and are involved in the work of mentoring others.

Everyone in the body of Christ fits into one of these spiritual categories, but the fewest number will be found in the "father" class. Paul acknowledged this when he said, "For though you might have ten thousand instructors in Christ, yet you do not have many fathers..." (1 Cor. 4:15).

CHARACTERISTICS OF CHILDREN

John not only cites the existence of these three levels of spiritual maturity, but he also lists the identifying characteristics of each one.

"I write to you, little children, because your sins are forgiven you for His name's sake" (v. 12)

When people come to Christ, the first (and sometimes just about the only) thing they know is that their sins are forgiven. They revel in God's forgiveness and possess a childlike wonder about the power of the name that set them free. They may not understand too much about other spiritual truths or how the kingdom operates, but they know that they are saved.

A while back, at one of my son's basketball games, a gentleman came up to me and introduced himself. Less than a month earlier, he had been saved at our church out of a life of drugs and despair. He was filled with joy, wonder, and thankfulness in his newfound life with Christ. He was so typical of a new babe in Christ: full of questions, wanting to know what God required of him, but, most of all, he just talked about Jesus. No matter where our conversation went, he kept bringing it back to Jesus, wonderful Jesus.

At one point, he almost started crying as he expressed his amazement over the humility of Christ. I thoroughly enjoyed my time with that precious brother. He really challenged me to keep the fires of my first love burning brightly within my heart. When your sins are forgiven and you understand the grace of God that set you free from captivity, then joy and amazement consume your life.

John went on to say, "...I write to you, little children, because you have known the Father" (v. 13). He wrote this because Christianity all boils down to relationship. According to Jesus, that is the essence of eternal life. (John 17:3.) It is the core of Christianity. Although spiritual children may not have a deep grasp of the Bible's theology, they do know that their sins are forgiven and that they have a relationship with the Father.

CHARACTERISTICS OF YOUNG MEN

Next, John writes to the young men, who are more spiritually mature and have grown in knowledge. "...I have written to you, young men, because you are strong, and the word of God abides in you, and you have overcome the wicked one" (1 John 2:14).

Those belonging to this group have the Word abiding in them. They are gaining victories and going forward in the Lord, possessing their inheritance. They know that they have authority over Satan. They know they have rights and privileges as believers. They are strong in the Lord and can share with others God's principles of faith. They have been through spiritual conflict and tasted victory. They are very keen on finding and possessing all that belongs to them in Christ.

CHARACTERISTICS OF FATHERS

Then John addresses the most seasoned believers, those belonging to the class of fathers. "I write to you, fathers, because you have known Him who is from the beginning..." (v. 13). "I have written to you, fathers, because you have known Him who is from the beginning..." (v. 14). John states the exact same thing twice. Why? To emphasize its importance, just as Joseph told Pharaoh concerning his dreams, "it was repeated...twice because the thing is established by God" (Gen. 41:32). It would behoove us to pay special attention to this identifying quality of spiritual fathers.

Amazingly enough, the thing that identifies the father in 1 John 2 is the same thing the Lord said about the children! "...I write to you, little children, because you have known the Father" (v. 13). The exact same Greek word is used for "known" (*ginosko*: knowledge obtained, not by mere intellect, but by operation of the Holy Spirit) in the case of both the children and the father.

The father in the Lord knows doctrine and how to possess his inheritance, just as the young man does. He knows that Satan is defeated, and he understands how kingdom principles operate—but he has come to realize that possessing the promises is not the most important thing. He also realizes that gaining victories and exercising authority, though vital, are not the paramount issue. The father realizes that there is something of far greater value than all these things—relationship.

In fact, relationship with God is the source from which all these things get their life. The simplicity of walking with God and knowing Him more intimately is the father's chief desire. Everything else pales in comparison with the wonder of knowing Him!

KNOWING GOD

Knowing God is a lifelong pursuit. The more you know Him, the more you want to know Him. When Saul of Tarsus had his conversion experience on the Damascus Road, he asked the Lord two questions. Number one: "Who are You, Lord?" Number two: "Lord, what do You want me to do?" (Acts 9:5,6.) And from that day on Paul's life revolved around progressively finding the answers to those two questions.

Well over twenty years later, in his epistle to the Philippians, we see Paul still passionately pursuing the answers to these fundamental questions. Listen to his heart cry as he puts ink to paper while locked up in a Roman prison cell: "…that I may know Him and…. I press on, that I may lay hold of that for which Christ Jesus has also laid hold of me" (Phil. 3:10,12). Paul was a father in the Lord who knew the importance of not just maintaining but growing in his relationship with the Lord.

My wife, Janet, and I recently went out to dinner with a young woman who is being greatly used in ministry today. As we sat talking about the things of God, she asked what had kept us on track with God these last ten years. Others have become jaded or drifted away from their original calling, so she basically said, "I see you guys are still in love with Jesus, preaching the gospel, and having a tremendous impact in what you do. What's your secret?"

I borrowed a Bible from someone at the table and opened to 1 John 2:12-14. After reading these verses and pointing out that the spiritual father's passion is the same as the spiritual children's, I said, "We've stayed on track because we continue to stay thankful for our salvation, and our relationship with God is our number one priority. It's that simple. The things that we did in the beginning we are still doing now."

DANGERS FOR YOUNG MEN TO AVOID

If not careful, Christians in the category of young men can drift away from their first love until their life becomes one of working principles. Getting things *from* and doing things *for* God end up as their focus, but they lose sight of the heart of Christianity and salvation, which is *knowing* God.

Fathers must—more than anything else—model a walking, talking, living, breathing relationship with the Father. We need their pattern and wisdom. There is a real danger when, either by our choice or due to scarcity, there are no spiritual fathers in our lives. I know many young men with growing churches and ministries who are bringing millions of dollars into the kingdom, constructing buildings, getting on radio and TV, and preaching in great crusades, but they are surrounded only by their peers! They are young lions getting counsel *only* from other young lions and are held accountable *only* to others in their group.

I even heard one young man with a growing ministry say, "Only when your church is as big as mine or when you have done what I've done will I listen to you. Otherwise, don't bother trying. You have nothing to say to me." What an arrogant and prideful posture to take! To think that someone who has been in the ministry decades longer than you has nothing of value to say simply because his or her church or ministry is not as large as yours is foolishness!

REHOBOAM'S COUNSELORS

Men like that are making the same mistake that young King Rehoboam made when he took over the kingdom from his father, Solomon.

> **...The whole assembly of Israel came and spoke to Rehoboam, saying, "Your father made our yoke heavy; now therefore, lighten the burdensome service of your father, and his heavy yoke which he put on us, and we will serve you." So he said to them, "Depart for three days, then come back to me." And the**

people departed. Then King Rehoboam consulted the elders who stood before his father Solomon while he still lived, and he said, "How do you advise me to answer these people?" And they spoke to him, saying, "If you will be a servant to these people today, and serve them, and answer them, and speak good words to them, then they will be your servants forever." But he rejected the advice which the elders had given him, and consulted the young men who had grown up with him, who stood before him. And he said to them, "What advice do you give? How should we answer this people who have spoken to me, saying, 'Lighten the yoke which your father put on us'?"

Then the young men who had grown up with him spoke to him, saying, "Thus you should speak to this people who have spoken to you, saying, 'Your father made our yoke heavy, but you make it lighter on us'—thus you shall say to them: 'My little finger shall be thicker than my father's waist! And now, whereas my father laid a heavy yoke on you, I will add to your yoke; my father chastised you with whips, but I will chastise you with scourges!' " So Jeroboam and all the people came to Rehoboam the third day, as the king had directed, saying, "Come back to me the third day." Then the king answered the people roughly, and rejected the advice which the elders had given him; and he spoke to them according to the advice of the young men, saying, "My father made your yoke heavy, but I will add to your yoke; my father chastised you with whips, but I will chastise you with scourges!"

1 Kings 12:3-14

One minister whom I know—and have greatly admired for all he has achieved—made some decisions to change how he would conduct a certain aspect of his ministry. I personally thought it was a bad choice and could have put a "sour taste" in the mouths of people who were looking to his ministry for spiritual guidance and nourishment. His reasoning was, "I talked to So-and-So, and I ran it by So-and-So, and I asked So-and-So, and they all agreed. So it has to be of God." It's true that "…in the multitude of counselors there is safety" (Prov. 11:14). But every person he mentioned, like himself, was in the "young man" category (I knew most of them, personally). There wasn't a single "father" in the bunch.

I cherish and do everything I can to maintain the relationships I have with the spiritual fathers I know. I communicate with them and spend time with them whenever I can, and I can truly say that they have "saved my bacon" a time or two with the sagely advice they have given me. Relationships like these should never be taken for granted.

When I was first saved, one of the people who spiritually mentored me was a woman named Eva Phelps. She had known the Lord for over sixty years and graciously took me under her wing during that first period following my conversion. Eva taught me the way of the Spirit. She prayed for me and warned me about the importance of obeying God. There is no way I can truly estimate the impact that dear woman had on my life. In the process of time, I moved back to Southern California, where I had grown up, and I lost track of Eva.

Months turned into years, and I always had this gnawing thought in the back of my mind that I needed to contact her, but I failed to do so. Finally, after about three years, I realized what a fool I had been for not benefiting from the treasure in that great old saint of God. So I picked up the phone and called: "Hello." I recognized her husband's voice immediately.

"Hi, Fred. This is Bayless. How ya' doing? Is Eva there?"

"Oh, I guess you didn't hear," Fred said quietly. "Eva passed away about two months ago."

I was in shock, not only because a dear friend had passed away, but also because I had squandered one of the greatest resources I might ever find. Eva was gone. She was in heaven, and so was all of her wisdom and experience. I grieved for days, but not for Eva— she had gained heaven. I grieved for the loss of a true spiritual mentor and for my dullness in neglecting the opportunity to learn from her experience while she was here.

Because the words of Paul, "...you do not have many fathers..." (1 Cor. 4:15), are true, we should never treat lightly the great privilege of learning from someone who has been a forerunner in spiritual things. Young men need a father's wisdom to steady them and keep them on course. Children need a father's example and instruction to help them grow.

SIX LESSONS THAT SPIRITUAL CHILDREN NEED TO LEARN

Writing as a spiritual father in his first epistle, John addressed believers as little children in connection with six different issues. And in so doing, he revealed six lessons that all spiritual children must be taught if they are to grow and stay on course in the Lord. Let's look at each one of them.

Lesson Number 1: God is faithful and just to forgive.

> If we confess our sins, He is faithful and just to forgive us our sins and to cleanse us from all unrighteousness. If we say that we have not sinned, we make Him a liar, and His word is not in us.

> *1 John 1:9,10*

> My little children, these things I write to you, that you may not sin. And if anyone sins, we have an Advocate with the Father, Jesus Christ the righteous.

> *1 John 2:1*

> I write to you, little children, because your sins are forgiven you for His name's sake.

> *1 John 2:12*

If young believers are not taught about forgiveness, they will wallow in condemnation, feeling as if they have utterly failed God the first time they do something wrong. They need to know that, as far as sin goes, their past before Christ has been erased and that any sin committed after salvation, if confessed and repented of, is forgiven and forgotten by God.

I spoke with a young believer some time ago who was convinced that God no longer loved her because of some sin she had committed. The devil had her convinced that if she were "really saved," she wouldn't have done such an awful thing (I didn't even bother to ask what she had done). I quickly had her open her Bible to 1 John 1:9 and had her read it. "Are you sorry for what you did?" I asked.

"Oh, yes!" she said, with her head still hanging down.

"Have you confessed it to God?" I queried.

"Yes."

"Then He has already forgiven you."

"But has anyone else ever failed God like me?" she asked—sounding now a little bit hopeful.

"Look at 1 John 2:1," I said.

She slowly read it: "My little children, these things I write to you, that you may not sin. And if anyone sins, we have an Advocate with the Father, Jesus Christ the righteous."

After she read it, I asked, "Do you know who wrote this?"

"John did," she replied.

I explained: "Yes. The one we call the Apostle of Love. The one who had his head upon Jesus' breast at the Last Supper. The same one God used to write the Gospel of John, as well as four other books in the Bible. *That* John said, '...If anyone sins, we have an Advocate with the Father....' He didn't say you have an Advocate. He said *we*, including John himself. So I guess John needed the Lord's forgiveness sometimes too."

The young lady began to laugh. She saw it. "I never thought I would feel this way again," she said. We had a short time of prayer together. Then she went her way, smiling and restored to fellowship with God.

I was simply passing along to this young Christian what someone had shared with me as a young Christian. I had done something wrong, and my conscience immediately convicted me. I tried to pray, but my mind was flooded by odd portions of Scripture, such as this: "…Because you have rejected knowledge, I also will reject you from being priest for Me; because you have forgotten the law of your God, I also will forget your children" (Hos. 4:6). It's *over*, I thought. *God has forsaken me—and my children.*

I assumed that the Scriptures that were coming to me were from God, but, in reality, it was the devil talking to my mind. (Matt. 4:5-7.) I was literally being tormented. Then a friend walked up, set a Bible down in front of me, opened it to 1 John, chapter one, and verse nine was underlined in red ink: "If we confess our sins, He is faithful and just to forgive us our sins and to cleanse us from all unrighteousness." As I read it, relief flooded over my soul. God hadn't forsaken me! I could be forgiven. I learned a valuable lesson that day, one that every little child in the Lord needs to learn: God is faithful and just to forgive.

Lesson Number 2: Everything that glitters is not gold.

Little children, it is the last hour; and as you have heard that the Antichrist is coming, even now many antichrists have come, by which we know that it is the last hour. They went out from us, but they were not of us; for if they had been of us, they would have continued with us; but they went out that they might be made manifest, that none of them were of us. But you have an anointing from the Holy One, and you know all things. I have not written to you because you do not know the truth, but because you know it, and that no lie is of the truth. Who is a liar but he who denies that Jesus is the Christ? He is antichrist who denies the Father and the Son. Whoever denies the Son does not have the Father either; he who acknowledges the Son has the Father also.

Therefore let that abide in you which you heard from the beginning. If what you heard from the beginning abides in you, you also will abide in the Son and in the Father. And this is the promise that He has promised us—eternal life. These things I have written to you concerning those who try to deceive you. But the anointing which you have received from Him abides in you, and you do not need that anyone teach you; but as the same anointing teaches you concerning all things, and is true, and is not a lie, and just as it has taught you, you will abide in Him. And now, little children, abide in Him, that when He appears, we may have confidence and not be ashamed before Him at His coming.

1 John 2:18-28

There are plenty of deceivers in the world, and unfortunately, quite a few are dressed up in religious clothing. There are folks who know all the religious lingo and may have even "gone out from us," as John says. In other words, they've separated themselves from the rest of the body. But they were never really a part of Christ's body or they would have continued in fellowship with the local church. Spiritual children need to be taught that everything that glitters is not gold. There are wolves in sheep's clothing and ministers of Satan who transform themselves into the ministers of righteousness whom we must guard against. (2 Cor. 11:3.) In writing about the threat of those deceivers, John shares two principles, which, if followed, will keep spiritual children on course with God.

First, he emphasizes that we must stay with the foundational things that we have been taught. "Therefore let that abide in you which you heard from the beginning. If what you heard from the beginning abides in you, you also will abide in the Son and in the Father" (1 John 2:24).

One of the characteristics of both natural and spiritual children is that they get bored easily. Scores of immature believers flock to meetings in order to have a "new" experience or to hear some "new" slant on the truth. They tire of the "meat and potatoes" of the gospel and want something more exciting or "cutting edge." Dear friend, I am not against someone having an experience with the Holy Spirit, "falling under the power," or sharing some fresh insight from the Scriptures. If these things are of God, they will make us live holier lives and give us an increased passion to reach the lost. They will also help us to fall more in love with Jesus. But if these are not the results, then I doubt whether the experience or teaching is of God at all.

We are to always let the things we heard from the beginning abide in us. Never let the simple things like honoring God and helping people drift out of focus. Don't get lured away from the bedrock of going to church and sharing Christ with a lost and dying world. They may not be "new" concepts, but if you let them abide in you, you will abide in the Son and in the Father.

Second, John tells us that we must learn to listen to the inward anointing:

> **But you have an anointing from the Holy One, and you know all things.**
>
> **But the anointing which you have received from Him abides in you, and you do not need that anyone teach you; but as the same anointing teaches you concerning all things, and is true, and is not a lie, and just as it has taught you, you will abide in Him.**
>
> **1 John 2:20,27**

The "anointing" in this passage refers to the indwelling presence of God's Spirit. Whenever a person was anointed with oil in the Old Testament, it was symbolic of the Holy Spirit's presence coming upon them. Under the new covenant, the Holy Spirit no longer just comes upon us—He dwells within us. And now, from the inside, He teaches us all things. This is what Paul writes about in Romans 8:16, where he says, "The Spirit Himself bears witness with our spirit that we are children of God."

When people are saved, the Holy Spirit abides in them, bearing witness in their hearts that they have been changed and made a part of God's family. First John 5:10 says, "He who believes in the Son of God has the witness in himself...." In other words, the same unction of the Holy Spirit that let you know you were saved will let you distinguish between truth and deception!

In context, these verses about the anointing deal with recognizing deceivers and people who have a wrong spirit. This truth doesn't negate the need for guidance from pastors and other spiritual leaders in the body. It simply emphasizes the fact that spiritual children need to be taught to recognize the inward prompting of the Holy Spirit. If they can recognize that they are saved, they can recognize truth from error in the same way.

Years ago I heard an older minister relate a story about a woman he had known. At the time, she and her family were all new converts attending a good, Spirit-filled church in their town. The pastor, though at times leaning more to his intellect than to his heart, was a good Bible teacher, and the lady and her family were quite happy there.

One day an unknown minister turned up in town and advertised that he was having Bible meetings. The first night, the pastor went by himself to investigate and was captivated by this man's teaching. He was brilliant, and because the pastor was very intellectually inclined, he enjoyed the man's thinking and insights. So the next day, he gathered about thirty or so of his people to attend the nightly meetings. This woman, a new convert, and her family were among those who attended.

But something was wrong. All through the meeting, something bothered her inside. At first she thought, *I'm just judging him.* But then she realized it wasn't that. Something in her spirit was bothered by this new Bible teacher. As hard as she tried, she couldn't escape the agitated feeling she experienced inside as she listened to this man speak.

Following the meeting, she shared her apprehensions with the pastor, and he assured her that everything was all right. But she persisted, "Pastor, I don't know what it is, but I feel uneasy inside.

If it's all right with you, my family and I won't be attending any more of these meetings."

"That's fine," replied the pastor, "but I don't believe anything is wrong."

As the nightly meetings progressed, the man seemed to use less and less of the Bible and even began to contradict certain areas of Scripture. Finally, one evening after the man had blatantly taught something that was unscriptural, this pastor approached him. "Sir, you know that my people and I have been attending your meetings every night, and you have shared some good things. There have been a few things that I didn't agree with, but what you taught tonight is absolutely unscriptural. I'd like you to give me chapter and verse for the statements you made."

"Chapter and verse?" the man inquired. "I don't need the Bible. I'm way beyond that thing."

The pastor was stunned. He realized that this man was a false teacher, but it was too late. Though he tried to pull his people out, some of them stayed on and continued going to these meetings, eventually leaving his church altogether.

Why did that new convert recognize this man as a deceiver while her pastor did not? Because she was listening to the Holy Spirit's inward prompting while the pastor was only listening to his head.

I read of a similar incident regarding a minister with a new convert on the streets of Los Angeles. As they walked, they came upon a man preaching on a street corner. He sounded very convincing, but the older minister recognized immediately that he was a member of a non-Christian cult. They listened for about ten minutes. Then as they walked away, the minister, somewhat concerned that this new convert had been taken in by this street preacher asked, "What did you think of him?"

"Well," responded the young man, "a lot of what he said seemed to make sense. But the whole time he was speaking, something inside of me kept saying, 'Liar! Liar!'" That something inside of him was the anointing.

Lesson Number 3: Lifestyle is indicative of true spirituality.

> And you know that He was manifested to take away our sins, and in Him there is no sin. Whoever abides in Him does not sin. Whoever sins has neither seen Him nor known Him. Little children, let no one deceive you. He who practices righteousness is righteous, just as He is righteous. He who sins is of the devil, for the devil has sinned from the beginning. For this purpose the Son of God was manifested, that He might destroy the works of the devil. Whoever has been born of God does not sin, for His seed remains in him; and he cannot sin, because he has been born of God. In this the children of God and the children of the devil are manifest: Whoever does not practice righteousness is not of God, nor is he who does not love his brother.
>
> 1 John 3:5-10

When this passage proclaims that those abiding in Him do not sin, it is speaking about a habit of life. *The Amplified Bible* makes that clear:

> No one who abides in Him [who lives and remains in communion with and in obedience to Him—deliberately, knowingly, and habitually] commits (practices) sin. No one who [habitually] sins has either seen or known Him [recognized, perceived, or understood Him, or has had an experiential acquaintance with Him].
>
> No one born (begotten) of God [deliberately, knowingly, and habitually] practices sin, for God's nature abides in him [His principle of life, the divine sperm, remains permanently within him]; and he cannot practice sinning because he is born (begotten) of God.
>
> 1 John 3:6,9 AMP

The message is clear. When a person is saved, their lifestyle of sin stops. "If anyone is in Christ, he is a new creation..." (2 Cor. 5:17), and that new creation "...delights in the law of

God…" (Rom. 7:22), not in sin. Unquestionably, Christians do sin, but the more they grow in God, the fewer and farther between those sins become. So as far as a lifestyle of habitual sin is concerned, that ends when they give their hearts to Christ.

Years ago I was working out in a local gym. The regular people there were talking about the normal things they were interested in: sex, drugs, and parties. I was working out on a machine next to three guys who were engrossed in a story that one of them was telling. Hearing them was unavoidable because they were laughing and talking quite loudly.

As a young man finished telling about having sex with a girl in the backseat of his car in a nightclub parking lot, one of them looked up and noticed me. "You better shut up, man," he told his friend. "This guy is a Christian." Then something I wasn't prepared for happened. The guy who had just finished proudly telling his friends of his recent "conquest" blurted out, "Well, I'm a Christian, too!" I thought, *Oh, please! It would be better for you to tell people you are an atheist and witness in reverse!*

Listen, friend, just because you say you're a Christian doesn't make you one. Just because you go to church doesn't make you a Christian. Just because you've been baptized in water doesn't make you a Christian. Jesus said you must be born again! And if there truly has been a new birth, there eventually will be fruit to prove it. Jesus said, "Therefore by their fruits you will know them. Not everyone who says to Me, 'Lord, Lord' shall enter the kingdom of heaven, but he who does the will of My Father in heaven" (Matt. 7:20,21).

What an important lesson for young Christians to learn. There are many who profess to know Christ, but in their works they deny Him. The way one lives is a revelation of whom he or she serves.

Lesson Number 4: We must love in deed, not just in word.

> **But whoever has this world's goods, and sees his brother in need, and shuts up his heart from him, how does the love of God abide in him? My little children, let us not love in word or in**

tongue, but in deed and in truth. And by this we know that we are of the truth, and shall assure our hearts before Him.

1 John 3:17-19

One distinguishing characteristic of children is that they are self-centered. So new believers should be admonished to express their Christianity through good works. Real Christianity puts on work clothes and isn't afraid to break a sweat or get dirty by helping people in practical ways. Whether it is giving people money to help pay their rent, picking up their kids from school, or helping them carry the groceries in, we need to love through our actions, not just in words.

You don't have to travel very far to find a need. We are surrounded every day by a sea of hurting people who are longing for a glimpse of something real. Their whole world could be changed by just one unselfish act of love.

Emma was confined to a wheelchair because her hands and legs were twisted from arthritis. She had been in a rest home for years, forgotten, like so many other lonely people. But one day was different. Two young men came by to visit her. "What do you want?" Emma snarled as she eyed her unexpected visitors.

"We're just here to read people Bible stories and to sing songs for anyone who is interested," one of the young men in blue jeans responded.

"Well, I'm not interested," Emma said. "Now go away and leave me alone!"

The young men seemed surprised, but they smiled and said, "Okay, God bless you!" Then they proceeded down the hall to find someone who would be more accommodating. Two days later, however, they were back. "Hi, Emma! Interested in a Bible story today, or just care to visit?"

"No. Leave me alone," she snapped. "I don't want to visit, and I don't want to hear about God!"

"Okay, Emma. See you later," they would always say before going their way up and down the hallways into the various rooms where they were greeted by eager, wrinkled faces. Emma had obviously had a hard life and was very bitter, but slowly she began to soften. Twice a week, every week, those two young men would come to that rest home and always pay a visit to Emma first. Many times it never got beyond a "How are you today, Emma?" or, "You look nice today, Emma," before she drove off the persistent young visitors. But they were always kind to her, no matter how she treated them.

After awhile, Emma began to look forward to their visits, and eventually, she even waited for them by her doorway in her wheelchair. She began to open up and talk and even smiled once or twice (which delighted the young men very much).

Then one day, almost a year after they had started coming to the rest home, it happened. As they came in the door, guitar in hand, ready to visit and sing some of the old hymns, such as "Bringing in the Sheaves" or "In the Garden," Emma was there in her spot, waiting for them. But today something was definitely different. Emma was smiling from ear to ear. She raised one of her gnarled hands toward the boys and said, "Aren't you going to ask me?"

"Ask you what, Emma?" they said.

"Ask me if I want to get saved?" she answered beaming.

"Well, do you?" they asked, totally stunned by the question.

"Yes, I do. I want Jesus to come into my heart today."

The three of them prayed together, and Emma was gloriously saved. From that day on, she was the kindest, most tenderhearted person you would ever want to meet. Rarely, if ever, did the young men catch her without a smile on her face. Emma was won, not by word alone, but by deed.

That was over twenty years ago, but it has been etched into my memory because I was one of those young men.

When we get out and begin to touch people and help them in practical ways, it gives substance to our message. As children of God, we need to let our light shine before men that they may see our good works and, in response, glorify our Father in heaven.

Lesson Number 5: You need not fear the devil.

> **Beloved, do not believe every spirit, but test the spirits, whether they are of God; because many false prophets have gone out into the world. By this you know the Spirit of God: Every spirit that confesses that Jesus Christ has come in the flesh is of God, and every spirit that does not confess that Jesus Christ has come in the flesh is not of God. And this is the spirit of the Antichrist, which you have heard was coming, and is now already in the world. You are of God, little children, and have overcome them, because He who is in you is greater than he who is in the world.**

> **1 John 4:1-4**

Even the least member of the body of Christ has complete authority over the devil. Jesus has already defeated Satan and given the keys of authority to us. In His name, we are to cast out demons. The greater One is living in us, and through Christ, He has already overcome every "antichrist" spirit (any spirit that is against Christ).

Many new Christians, however, live in fear of the devil. The one thing that will liberate them from that fear is knowledge of the truth. It is imperative that we tell the little children of Christ's victory over every form of darkness. Young Christians must understand that, because Christ lives in them, they are victorious as well.

Years ago, a man who came out of a biker background came to Christ in one of our services. He had lived on the street since he was a boy and had been a pretty tough character. But he had a genuine conversion experience and began to attend church regularly. One evening after being saved a few weeks, he went out to a downtown area with a team from our church to share the gospel. He was passing out tracts along with everyone else when he came up to a little old lady. As he prepared to tell her about Jesus and give her a tract, she suddenly turned toward him, eyes bulging, and began speaking in a guttural, male-sounding voice. Webster's dictionary defines guttural as "of or relating to the throat; produced in the throat." She was possessed, and the demon in her began to manifest.

As this man related this story to me the next day, I said, "What did you do?"

"I ran away from her as fast as I could!" he answered.

I started laughing. The picture of this big biker running away from a little old lady was too much for me! "Listen, brother," I told him, "You don't need to be afraid of the devil! If anything like that ever happens again, stand your ground and command the evil spirit to come out in Jesus' name. The Bible says if we resist the devil, he will flee from us. We are not supposed to flee from him!" (James 4:7.)

Lesson Number 6: Idolatry is a real danger.

Little children, keep yourselves from idols. Amen.

1 John 5:21

Today most people's concept of idolatry is quite limited. When many people think of idolatry, they picture someone kneeling in a shrine and praying to some sort of carved image. But the biblical concept is far broader than that. To God, anything that comes before Him becomes an idol. *The Living Bible* translation of 1 John 5:21 reads, "Dear children, keep away from anything that might take God's place in your hearts. Amen."

The Scripture speaks of covetousness as being a form of idolatry. (Col. 3:5.) Paul talked about those "...whose god is their belly..." (Phil. 3:19). Quite literally, almost anything can become an idol: money, food, sports, the desire for comfort, a boyfriend, a girlfriend, your children, your spouse, yourself, your work, your ambition. We must constantly guard our hearts so that nothing comes before our relationship with God. Spiritual children, in particular, need to be warned of the danger of idolatry.

Some time ago, I was listening as a professional golfer was being interviewed about his career. He had made millions of dollars on the PGA Tour and was, at the time of his interview, experiencing great success on the Senior PGA Tour. He said, "I have had a love affair with the game of golf. It has come before everyone and everything else in my life. It cost me my marriage to my first wife and my relationship with my children. In fact, even today, now that they are grown, I'm still not close to them. Golf has become my god."

The interviewer then asked him a very piercing question: "If you had it all to do over again, would you do it differently?" Without hesitation, he said, "No, I'd do just the same." Idolatry! He had laid the most valuable things he had on the altar of his god and sacrificed them.

Little children, keep yourselves from idols.

THE RESPONSIBILITY TO GROW

Every Christian has the responsibility to feed upon the pure milk of God's Word in order to grow spiritually. (1 Peter 2:2.) Babyhood is unavoidable—there are no shortcuts to spiritual maturity—but if we are to grow as Christians, we must will to grow. We must do what is necessary so God's maturation process can take place in our lives. May we not be like those the writer of Hebrews talked about when he said, "For though by this time you ought to be teachers, you need someone to teach you again the first principles of the oracles of God; and you have come to need milk and not solid food" (Heb. 5:12).

Aspire to spiritual maturity. Involve yourself in the necessary disciplines of study, prayer, fellowship, and church attendance so you can grow up in the Lord. Make the decision that the day will come when you will be the one helping someone else grow. Choose early that one day it will be your hand steadying a spiritual toddler in his walk with the Lord.

"MY THREE SONS"

I do not write these things to shame you, but as my beloved children I warn you. For though you might have ten thousand instructors in Christ, yet you do not have many fathers; for in Christ Jesus I have begotten you through the gospel. Therefore I urge you, imitate me. For this reason I have sent Timothy to you, who is my beloved and faithful son in the Lord, who will remind you of my ways in Christ, as I teach everywhere in every church.

1 Corinthians 4:14-17

Although there were not many fathers in Paul's day, Paul was a father to many. He refers to the entire Corinthian church as his "beloved children." He calls the saints at Galatia his "little children." (Gal. 4:19). He speaks to the Thessalonian believers "…as a father does his own children" (1 Thess. 2:11). Yet in all of his writings, Paul specifically calls only three individuals his sons by name: Timothy, Titus, and Onesimus.

As we examine the relationship between the apostle and his "three sons," we find six principles that serve as a standard for each of us as we endeavor to mentor those whom the Lord has entrusted to our care. In this chapter, I will discuss each of them with the aim of equipping you, as a spiritual father, with more wisdom from Paul.

1. He delivered them.

Even as a woman *delivers* her child when her time is due, Paul, through preaching the gospel, brought each of these men into a new birth experience and so became their father in the Lord.

TIMOTHY

Timothy was most likely converted during Paul's first missionary journey as he preached the gospel in the cities of Lystra and Derbe. Upon returning to those same cities to confirm the churches during his second missionary journey, Paul was accompanied by Timothy, who was well spoken of by the brethren there. (Acts 16:1-3,6,7.)

TITUS

We are not told exactly how or when Titus came to the Lord—only that Paul refers to him as "...a true son in our common faith" (Titus 1:4).

ONESIMUS

The story of Onesimus is very interesting indeed when you discover *how* the apostle led him to Christ, and *where*. Let's read his story:

> **Therefore, though I might be very bold in Christ to command you what is fitting, yet for love's sake I rather appeal to you—being such a one as Paul, the aged, and now also a prisoner of Jesus Christ—I appeal to you for my son Onesimus, whom I have begotten while in my chains, who once was unprofitable to you, but now is profitable to you and to me. I am sending him back. You therefore receive him, that is, my own heart, whom I wished to keep with me, that on your behalf he might**

minister to me in my chains for the gospel. But without your consent I wanted to do nothing, that your good deed might not be by compulsion, as it were, but voluntary.

For perhaps he departed for a while for this purpose, that you might receive him forever, no longer as a slave but more than a slave—a beloved brother, especially to me but how much more to you, both in the flesh and in the Lord. If then you count me as a partner, receive him as you would me. But if he has wronged you or owes anything, put that on my account. I, Paul, am writing with my own hand. I will repay—not to mention to you that you owe me even your own self besides. Yes, brother, let me have joy from you in the Lord; refresh my heart in the Lord. Having confidence in your obedience, I write to you, knowing that you will do even more than I say.

Philemon 1:8-21

Onesimus was the slave of a wealthy Christian named Philemon, who was also one of Paul's converts. Apparently, Onesimus had stolen some of his master's money and fled to Rome, where he hoped to get lost among the thronging masses of that great city. As so often happens, his plans didn't unfold as he had hoped. Something went wrong and Onesimus ended up in a jail cell next to some "religious fanatic" named Paul. This fanatic was constantly talking about someone named Jesus and "God's way to salvation."

Onesimus might have protested, but the Roman guards had just been converted themselves and they urged him to listen to Paul. Eventually, the eyes of this runaway slave began to open and he, too, gave his heart to Christ. And when he did, he was thoroughly changed.

Even after his release, Onesimus did everything he could to serve this man who had "begotten him through the gospel." (1 Cor. 4:15.) Although the ministry of this new son was a comfort to Paul, the apostle thought it better that things be reconciled between Onesimus and Philemon. So Paul sent Onesimus back to Philemon in

Colosse and the church in his house, carrying the letter that is now part of the New Testament.

PAUL MADE THE BEST OF EVERY OPPORTUNITY

Whether he was visiting a local synagogue, addressing Greek philosophers on the Areopagus, or sitting chained in a Roman prison cell, Paul was always engaged in the business of winning souls. He made the best of every opportunity and had many sons in the Lord as a result of first winning them to Christ. Sometimes they were birthed under the most adverse conditions.

In whatever circumstances you find yourself today, however difficult things may seem, God can still use you—if you will make yourself available. Don't wait for perfect conditions before you sow your seed. Plant the gospel in someone's heart today. You may be surprised. Some of God's greatest treasures are found during difficult times and in unusual places.

2. He deposited into them.

The second principle we learn through Paul's three sons is "deposit." Paul deposited himself into the lives of these young men via the letters that bear their names and through associating with them in prayer and in personal ministry.

> **This charge I commit to you, son Timothy, according to the prophecies previously made concerning you, that by them you may wage the good warfare.**
>
> **1 Timothy 1:18**

> **Do not neglect the gift that is in you, which was given to you by prophecy with the laying on of the hands of the eldership. Meditate on these things; give yourself entirely to them, that your progress may be evident to all.**
>
> **1 Timothy 4:14,15**

Although it is likely that Paul was present and played an active part during the particular times of personal ministry mentioned in

Timothy's letter, we can't know for sure. It may have only happened under the leadership of the elders he appointed during his first missionary journey.

Whatever the case, he was obviously aware of it and acknowledged its validity. One way or the other, Paul understood that a gift was deposited in Timothy through the means of prophetic ministry. In 2 Timothy, Paul goes on to refer to times when he personally prayed for and ministered to his son through the laying on of hands:

> **I thank God, whom I serve with a pure conscience, as my forefathers did, as without ceasing I remember you in my prayers night and day, greatly desiring to see you, being mindful of your tears, that I may be filled with joy, when I call to remembrance the genuine faith that is in you, which dwelt first in your grandmother Lois and your mother Eunice, and I am persuaded is in you also. Therefore I remind you to stir up the gift of God which is in you through the laying on of my hands.**
>
> 2 Timothy 1:3-6

As I shared earlier, when I was first saved, there was a dear old saint named Eva who took me under her wing. She had walked with Christ for more than sixty years. Not only did she pray for me daily but also, on several occasions, Eva laid hands on me and ministered through prophetic utterance. I can honestly say that I don't believe I would be where I am today had she not deposited into my life. Eva was truly a mother in the Lord.

FAMILY REUNION

Because of my drug use and crazy lifestyle, relations with my family had been severely strained prior to my salvation. The last several years that I lived at home took their toll on my parents. They constantly worried over whether or not I would live through another day. I wouldn't turn up for days at a time. Then when I did, I was usually either drunk or high on drugs. I later moved to Oregon (my parents lived in Southern California) and continued with my drug and alcohol abuse for several more years.

Once I was saved and set free, things were not restored with my family. I hadn't had any relationship with them or really seen them for more than four years. Then one night as I was attending a Full Gospel Business Men's dinner, I ran into Eva and her husband, Fred.

The moment Eva saw me, she grabbed my hands, put her wrinkled face a couple of inches from mine and began to prophesy: "Things aren't right between you and your family. God wants to restore your relationship with your family. Things aren't right…you need to go home!" The instant she began to speak, God's presence fell on me like a blanket from heaven. Eva hadn't known a thing about my family situation. But God did, and I knew He was speaking to me.

Two days later, I called my parents. My mother, who had recently been saved, answered the phone. "Hello?"

"…Uh…hi, Mom. It's me. Would it be okay with you and Dad if I came home?" I wasn't sure whether they'd want me or not, but without hesitation, my mom said, "Yes, and I've got something to tell you when you get here."

I sold my guitar at a local pawnshop for gas money, and rolled into my parents' driveway in my '63 Volkswagen microbus twenty-four hours later. Before I even entered the house, my mom told me this story:

Several days before (I believe it was the same day that Eva had prophesied to me about coming home), my mother was attending a Christian gathering in Anaheim, California. Right in the middle of the preacher's sermon, he had stopped and said, "The Lord just told me that there is a lady here who hasn't seen her son in about four years. He was on drugs and got involved in worse things after that (which was true), but he has been saved. His life has turned around, and he's coming home. It's already done in the Spirit."

My mother elbowed the lady next to her and said, "That's my son!" She went home and told my dad what had happened, to which he replied very matter-of-factly, "It'd take a miracle." And he was right!

The relationship with my family was restored. Everyone is now saved, and my parents, my sister, and her husband and children all attend the church I pastor!

I will be forever grateful to the Lord for all He has done. And I will always be thankful for an elderly saint named Eva, who prayed for me night and day, and deposited into me through personal ministry.

3. He duplicated himself in them.

The third principle we learn through Paul's three sons is "duplication." Paul duplicated himself in the life of his sons. Through the power of association, his lifestyle, values, and even his attitudes were transmitted to these men. His life became a blueprint for them to follow.

> **But you have carefully followed my doctrine, manner of life, purpose, faith, longsuffering, love, perseverance, persecutions, afflictions, which happened to me at Antioch, at Iconium, at Lystra—what persecutions I endured. And out of them all the Lord delivered me.**
>
> 2 Timothy 3:10,11

In studying these verses, I found that the phrase translated *carefully followed* means "to trace out a pattern." Paul was literally a living blueprint that his sons in the faith could follow. Every aspect of his walk with God was purposely laid out for these young men to understand and imitate. I can just imagine some of the late-night conversations they must have had as Paul endeavored to make plain his goals, motives, and methods. Perhaps they shared seasons of prayer together, during which these young apprentices heard their father in the faith pour out his heart to God.

I can imagine them listening and agreeing intently as he made supplication for the churches and prayed concerning his own trials and challenges. Through their interaction, Paul made the *lines of his life* bold and clear so that his sons in the Lord could trace the pattern.

LIKE-MINDED

But I trust in the Lord Jesus to send Timothy to you shortly, that I also may be encouraged when I know your state. For I have no one like-minded, who will sincerely care for your state. For all seek their own, not the things which are of Christ Jesus. But you know his proven character, that as a son with his father he served with me in the gospel.

Philippians 2:19-22

Timothy and Paul were like-minded. They shared the same spirit and attitudes because "...as a son with his father, [Timothy] served with me in the gospel."

My sons have adopted many of my characteristics through both observation and instruction. I remember when our eldest son, Harrison, was still a toddler. He was strapped into his car seat, sitting across from me in the front of the car. I had just spit out of the car window on the driver's side when I noticed that Harrison seemed to be studying me closely.

In a few seconds he turned toward his window and spit, only his window wasn't rolled down! He looked at me with a huge smile on his face that seemed to say, "Didn't I do good, Daddy? I'm just like you!" He was tracing out the pattern he had seen! Needless to say, such incidents have helped me to change a few of my old habits.

Sons will copy their fathers. They will adopt values and attitudes that are similar, if not identical, to those of their perceived role models. Timothy was blessed to have a mentor like Paul, and Paul was blessed to have a like-minded and faithful son like Timothy to labor alongside him in the ministry.

TITUS

Now for the third time I am ready to come to you. And I will not be burdensome to you; for I do not seek yours, but you. For the children ought not to lay up for the parents, but the parents for the children. And I will very gladly spend and be spent for your souls; though the more abundantly I love you, the less I am loved.

But be that as it may, I did not burden you. Nevertheless, being crafty, I caught you by cunning! Did I take advantage of you by any of those whom I sent to you? I urged Titus, and sent our brother with him. Did Titus take advantage of you? Did we not walk in the same spirit? Did we not walk in the same steps? Again, do you think that we excuse ourselves to you? We speak before God in Christ. But we do all things, beloved, for your edification.

2 Corinthians 12:14-19

As with Timothy, Paul was confident that Titus both conducted himself and made decisions that were consistent with his own heart because he had duplicated himself in the life of this son in the faith.

I am personally very grateful to God for the benefit of having like-minded people on our church team. I can rest easy, knowing that most of the decisions that are being made will be consistent with my heart and my vision.

One of the dangers of bringing in outside people to be a part of your church team (those that weren't raised up under the leadership of the church) is that even though they may be incredibly gifted, they may hold different values. They may also espouse different methods that are incompatible with your mission and the way you feel God is directing you to accomplish it. They may still "get the job done," getting from point A to point B, but the way they do it will create turmoil for you and for the rest of the team if their methods are not consistent with who you are.

Sometimes we can overlook the need for having a "kindred spirit" and hire someone based solely on his or her gifting or ability, resulting in a steady stream of turbulence.

To illustrate, I can think of a situation with which most of us are familiar. If you have ever flown on a plane and experienced turbulence due to the air currents, you know it isn't fun. You will reach your intended destination, but if there is a lot of turbulence throughout the trip, you will land wishing the pilot had taken a different route.

I have spoken in several churches where I have noticed right away a key person on the church staff with a "different spirit." Not that they were a bad or evil person—they may have been very gifted, even anointed, but they didn't walk in the same steps as the senior pastor. Their methods and manners conflicted with the person they were there to serve, and in most cases, there was turbulence. In fact, sometimes the turbulence was so great it seemed as if the ministry were going to shake apart.

Of course, there are exceptions to every rule. But generally, the best way to bring people up is through the ranks—people who have served and grown up in the Lord under your ministry. Overall, they make the best team members because they know your heart and have imbibed of your spirit and character.

The exception would be to bring in someone from the outside to join your leadership team. Although it is generally more difficult, it can work if the person coming on board is willing to adapt and learn to use his or her gifting in a way that doesn't violate your spirit or the spirit of your ministry.

4. He delegated to and released them.

Paul's fourth principle of spiritual fatherhood is "delegation." One of the purposes of raising up sons and daughters in the Lord is to help expand the work of the kingdom. Although some are faithful to raise others up, they often are not faithful to release them. But that was not the case with Paul.

ONESIMUS

Although Paul would have personally benefited from the ministry of Onesimus in Rome, he released him to be reconciled to Philemon in Colosse and to serve the church that met in his home.

According to Colossians 4:7-9, Onesimus was also sent along with Tychicus to comfort the believers at Colosse and to bring them news of Paul. (It is very likely that Onesimus carried the Colossian letter to the church there as well as carrying the letter bearing his name to Philemon.)

TITUS

Titus was entrusted by Paul to collect and transport large offerings from the Corinthian church to help suffering Christians elsewhere. (2 Cor. 8:6, 16-24.) But the great apostle also delegated several other demanding tasks to this son in the faith.

> **To Titus, a true son in our common faith: Grace, mercy, and peace from God the Father and the Lord Jesus Christ our Savior. For this reason I left you in Crete, that you should set in order the things that are lacking, and appoint elders in every city as I commanded you.**
>
> **Titus 1:4,5**

This was no easy task if you take into account what Paul said a few verses later:

> **One of them, a prophet of their own, said, "Cretans are always liars, evil beasts, lazy gluttons." This testimony is true. Therefore rebuke them sharply, that they may be sound in the faith.**
>
> **Titus 1:12,13**

Who would want to oversee that bunch? Paul knew that Titus was equal to the task. He had trained and poured into him, and now he was ready to be released. Why train someone if you never plan on releasing him or her? Why develop someone if you never delegate any responsibility or authority to him or her? To be trained and never used is not only a waste of effort and ability, it is disheartening to the one who has been prepared.

TIMOTHY

Like Titus, Timothy was a son in the faith who had been sown into and was finally ready to be "sown out into" the harvest field. Paul had given Timothy the responsibility of overseeing several churches. Both 1 and 2 Timothy are full of practical instructions on how he was to successfully accomplish that task.

He was also sent to the Christians in Thessalonica to establish and encourage them in the faith. (1 Thess. 3:1-7.) Releasing spiritual offspring into their own ministries—apart from the spiritual father's work—should also be included in this discussion. There are times when a spiritual father will be required to completely let go of the sons and daughters he has "raised up" in the Lord. God's grace is sufficient to cover the emotional loss you may experience because of your "investment" in those children.

Paul never tried to do it all himself. He often delegated things to his sons and sent them on important missions, trusting hundreds of converts into their care.

Our heart should be to see the work of God's kingdom expand, but that cannot happen if we don't delegate. We can't do it all, nor will God permit us to do it all. So we must raise up sons and daughters to help in our labor for the Lord.

I pastor a church with several thousand active members, so it is impossible for me to carry on the work alone. I cannot do all of the teaching, visitation, encouraging, etc. that needs to be done. If I tried to do it alone, it would only put me in an early grave. I have released a team of pastoral leaders to help me care for the flock. I have also been blessed with a large administrative staff and hundreds of volunteers who faithfully work toward the advancement of God's kingdom. It blesses me immeasurably to see someone on the team doing well or being greatly used by God. *That is what I want!*

Certainly there is the need for accountability, and we have certain mechanisms in place to accommodate that need. But I don't want to be guilty of training up people and then squelching their gifts because of my own ego or some personal insecurity. My job is not to train and restrain, but to increase and release.

5. He delighted in them and was devoted to them.

The fifth principle that Paul's fatherhood teaches us is "devotion." Paul never looked at these men as merely resources or tools to be used. They were his sons, and three of the chief delights of his heart. He told Philemon concerning Onesimus, "I am sending him—who is my very heart—back to you" (Philem. 1:12 NIV).

You can't read Paul's epistles to Timothy without feeling the deep bond between them. Look at the language he uses in 2 Timothy 1:2-5:

> **To Timothy, my beloved son: Grace, mercy, and peace from God the Father and Christ Jesus our Lord. I thank God, whom I serve with a pure conscience, as my forefathers did, as without ceasing I remember you in my prayers night and day, greatly desiring to see you, being mindful of your tears, that I may be filled with joy, when I call to remembrance the genuine faith that is in you, which dwelt first in your grandmother Lois and your mother Eunice, and I am persuaded is in you also.**

You can feel his emotion. You can see his heart. Paul loved Timothy.

When Paul came to Troas to preach, although the Lord had opened a door of ministry to him, he had no rest in his spirit because he didn't find Titus. (2 Cor. 2:12,13.)

He carried these men in his heart! They were tied to him, and he was tied to them. And so it is with every true spiritual father and the children he has poured his life into.

STEVE

Shortly after I was saved, I shared Christ with an old friend. We'll call him Steve. In the "old days," we used to drink and take drugs together. He showed no interest in the gospel when I initially talked to him. But I was burdened for his soul, so I continued to speak to him about Jesus whenever I had the opportunity. I also prayed for him regularly.

During that time the local college was planning to host a free concert by a Christian band, so I invited Steve. He thanked me for the invitation, but indicated that he had better things to do. So I went to the concert, which had about two hundred other people attending. After about an hour and a half of music, one of the band members invited the audience to accept Christ. The whole place grew silent as one lone figure from the back of the auditorium rose to his feet and began to make his way forward.

He was sobbing so violently that he looked as though he might collapse. When he finally reached the front, a Christian worker embraced him. He continued to cry for several more minutes, and, eventually, he prayed and received Christ as his Savior that night. I was filled with an indescribable sense of awe mingled with joy at the sight of it, because the one person who responded to the invitation that night was my friend, Steve.

Sometime during the concert he had slipped in the back. God answered my prayer, but my job had only begun.

MENTORING A NEW CONVERT

Although I hadn't been saved long myself, I began to teach Steve everything I knew about the Lord. We spent many hours studying the Bible together. I even had the privilege of laying hands on him to receive the Holy Spirit. In many ways, I looked at our new spiritual relationship as a father/son situation. I didn't know much, but I imparted what I knew. And I continued to pray for him.

All was well for a season, until a girl from Steve's past suddenly appeared on the scene. The more time he spent with her, the more his relationship with Christ deteriorated. I watched some of his old sinful patterns begin to creep back into his life, and, eventually, it came to the point where we parted ways.

When Steve began to fall away from his relationship with Jesus, it felt as though my very heart was being ripped out. I was tied to him. I had an instrumental part in bringing him to Christ. I had poured my life into him, and it had been the delight of my heart to watch him grow in the Lord. It wasn't something I could just disengage myself from.

Twenty-five years have come and gone since my ministry to Steve, and I still think of him fairly often. I still pray for him. I don't know where he is or what his life is like, but I can't forget about "my son in the Lord."

Mothers and fathers in Christ are devoted to their children. They "...have no greater joy than to hear that [their] children walk in truth" (3 John 4). At the same time, however, there is no greater sorrow than to know that one of your spiritual children has strayed from the path.

6. He depended on them to become fathers themselves.

The final principle of spiritual fatherhood drawn from the apostle Paul's mentoring experience with his three sons is "dependence." Paul sent his sons on important missions that involved delivering his letters, overseeing churches, and handling large sums of money. But more importantly than any of those things, he depended on them to reproduce themselves in others as he had done in them. If they had failed to do this, the work would have died with them!

Look with me at Paul's admonitions to Timothy:

> **Let no one despise your youth, but be an example to the believers in word, in conduct, in love, in spirit, in faith, in purity.**
>
> **1 Timothy 4:12**

Take heed to yourself and to the doctrine. Continue in them, for in doing this you will save both yourself and those who hear you.

1 Timothy 4:16

You therefore, my son, be strong in the grace that is in Christ Jesus. And the things that you have heard from me among many witnesses, commit these to faithful men who will be able to teach others also.

2 Timothy 2:1,2

In other words, "Timothy, reproduce in others what has been produced in you!"

Paul basically tells Titus the same thing in Titus 2:7-8: "...in all things showing yourself to be a pattern of good works; in doctrine showing integrity, reverence, incorruptibility, sound speech that cannot be condemned, that one who is an opponent may be ashamed, having nothing evil to say of you."

Among the greatest gifts you can give to a father are grandchildren. Proverbs 17:6 says, "Children's children are the crown of old men, and the glory of children is their father." When your spiritual children have children themselves, it is a crown of glory to you! A sense of godly pride is associated with that. When one of your sons or daughters in the Lord introduces their spiritual children to you, you know you've done your job well.

Success is not success without a successor. Your job, as a spiritual father or mother, is not finished until you produce spiritual offspring who are reproducing themselves in others.

Psalm 78:5-6 can be understood in the context of spiritual as well as natural offspring:

For He established a testimony in Jacob, and appointed a law in Israel, which He commanded our fathers, that they should make them known to their children; that the generation to come might know them, the children who would be born, that they may arise and declare them to their children.

The work of some of history's greatest preachers died with them because they failed to reproduce themselves in spiritual sons and daughters. They may have been brilliant in preaching to the masses. They may have consistently filled the land's largest auditoriums. But in the business of spiritual fathering, they were failures. And because of that, their work only flourished while they were alive.

In His great prayer just prior to His arrest and crucifixion, Jesus said, *"I have glorified You on the earth. I have finished the work which You have given Me to do"* (John 17:4). When Jesus made that statement, He wasn't talking about the work of redemption—He hadn't died on the cross yet.

Then we find in John 19:30 that Jesus cried, "It is finished!" just before He died. If Jesus wasn't referring to the work of redemption, to what work was He referring in John 17:4? It was the work of mentoring His disciples! He had spent nearly three and one-half years training and pouring Himself into them until they were ready to carry on His work. This is made quite clear in some of the following statements made by Jesus in the same prayer:

- "I have manifested Your name to the men whom You have given Me out of the world. They were Yours, You gave them to Me, and they have kept Your word. Now they have known that all things which You have given Me are from You. For I have given to them the words which You have given Me; and they have received them, and have known surely that I came forth from You; and they have believed that You sent Me. I pray for them. I do not pray for the world but for those whom You have given Me, for they are Yours" (vv. 6-9).

- "I have given them Your word; and the world has hated them because they are not of the world, just as I am not of the world" (v. 14).

- "As You sent Me into the world, I also have sent them into the world" (v. 18).

Had Jesus not mentored and prepared the disciples, God's message would have died with them! But because He poured into their lives, multitudes from every nation have believed on Him through their word: "I do not pray for these alone, but also for those who will believe in Me through their word" (v. 20).

With all of the strength and wisdom that God has given us, let us endeavor to raise an army of believers whose aim it is to grow spiritually and see the image of Christ in their own lives reproduced in others. Should Christ tarry, the salvation of this generation and the next is depending on it!

RESPONSIBILITIES OF SPIRITUAL CHILDREN

Just as natural children are not without responsibility in relation to their physical parents, spiritual children have certain responsibilities in relation to their spiritual parents. Although there may be more, I will discuss three primary responsibilities: first, honoring our spiritual fathers; second, putting into practice the truths they teach us; and third, surpassing their success.

1. Honor your father.

The first responsibility of spiritual children to their parents is honor.

> **Honor your father and your mother, as the Lord your God has commanded you, that your days may be long, and that it may be well with you in the land which the Lord your God is giving you.**
>
> **Deuteronomy 5:16**

This is number five in God's list of Ten Commandments. It was reiterated by Jesus on a number of occasions and quoted by Paul in Ephesians as being the first commandment with a promise. It addresses, of course, the responsibility of natural children toward their parents. But, in principle, it certainly could (and should) be applied to our spiritual mentors as well.

I have read that the Hebrew word translated *honor* in this verse means "to value or prize, to respect." But it also has another very significant shade of meaning: "to make weighty."[1] In other words, we should consider both the example and the sayings of our mentors very carefully. Their model of living and their words should be weighty to us—whether they bring guidance, correction, encouragement, or merely comfort. To treat their words or wisdom lightly is to *dishonor* them.

AN UNFORTUNATE PARALLEL

When natural children grow to be teenagers, they are notorious for thinking they "know it all." When that self-important age of thirteen is finally achieved, their parents, who have served as examples and teachers throughout their lives, suddenly become ignorant. The child who for so long looked to his parents for guidance and wisdom may no longer receive their instruction.

More often than not, we see an unfortunate parallel in the spiritual life. A young Christian begins to grow in knowledge and experience, and suddenly seems to get puffed up (1 Cor. 8:1), and no longer heeds the wisdom of his spiritual father. This is not only dishonoring and frustrating to the father, but it is also dangerous to the child.

The book of Proverbs sets out in crystal clarity the importance of heeding the wisdom of a father—and the dangers of neglecting to do so.

> **My son, hear the instruction of your father, and do not forsake the law of your mother.**
>
> **Proverbs 1:8**

> **Hear, my children, the instruction of a father, and give attention to know understanding; for I give you good doctrine: Do not forsake my law. When I was my father's son, tender and the only one in the sight of my mother, he also taught me, and said to me: "Let your heart retain my words; keep my commands, and live. Get wisdom! Get understanding! Do not forget, nor turn away from the words of my mouth."**

> **Proverbs 4:1-5**

> **A wise son heeds his father's instruction, but a scoffer does not listen to rebuke.**

> **Proverbs 13:1**

> **Listen to your father who begot you, and do not despise your mother when she is old.**

> **Proverbs 23:22**

To refuse to heed a father's instruction, or, worse yet, to let pride open the door to an arrogant or even hostile attitude, can result in disaster.

Naturally speaking, when I reached my teen years—especially around sixteen—I adopted an attitude that put me at odds with my father. I would listen to very little that he said. Sometimes, due to my pride and arrogance, things became so heated between us that hostile, angry words were spoken. My pride blinded me, and it took several years to discover that I had been the ignorant one and the major source of tension between us.

Spiritually speaking, to refuse to heed a father's instruction, or worse yet, to let pride open the door to an arrogant, hostile attitude, can bring on a state of spiritual blindness. And once you fall into this trap, you will find yourself in much pain, confusion, and heartache.

Some verses from Proverbs illustrate this truth well:

> **The spirit of a man is the lamp of the Lord, searching all the inner depths of his heart.**

> **Proverbs 20:27**

Whoever curses his father or his mother, his lamp will be put out in deep darkness.

Proverbs 20:20

God guides or enlightens you through your spirit. The spirit of man is the lamp of the Lord. But when bitterness or hostility exists between child and parent, that lamp is "put out" and can no longer illuminate the way. I believe this is the reason for some of the foolish decisions that are made by believers who should know better.

A person will make a choice or begin to follow a certain course of action that will obviously end in himself or others being hurt. And, as you watch him, your heart cries out: Why are you doing that? Can't you SEE that it is wrong? Don't you know you'll be hurt? Why can't you SEE it? The fact may be that he can't see it because his lamp isn't working properly.

Proverbs 30:17 illustrates this principle:

The eye that mocks his father, and scorns obedience to his mother, the ravens of the valley will pick it out, and the young eagles will eat it.

What an alarming picture! So it definitely pays to have a right relationship with both your earthly and spiritual parents—that is, unless you like walking in the dark!

2. Put into practice the truths that the father teaches.

The second responsibility of spiritual children to their parents is to practice what they teach.

I rejoiced greatly that I have found some of your children walking in truth, as we received commandment from the Father.

2 John 4

I have no greater joy than to hear that my children walk in truth.

3 John 4

The truth of God has to get beyond your ears and into your feet if it is ever going to profit you. I define the term walking here as "practicing." It is not good enough to merely hear, even if you agree. We must hear, agree, and do. Fathers don't rejoice in hearers of truth, or in those who merely agree with the truth. True spiritual fathers rejoice in doers of truth. The book of James goes so far as to declare that the one who merely hears the truth but never practices it is self-deceived. (James 1:22.)

A few years ago I attended a meeting for ministers in Southern California. As I was speaking to some pastors in the church lobby, a young man suddenly walked up to me and put out his hand. As I shook his hand, he looked me in the eye and asked, "Do you remember me?" His face triggered some faint memory, but I couldn't quite place him. "I'm Joe Delgado, and I met you in a meeting you were preaching in 1982." Suddenly, I remembered.

Joe was a high school kid who attended a series of meetings with his parents that I was preaching for a friend in Yucaipa, California. In one of those meetings, Joe received a miraculous healing. While ministering during that service, I looked over at this high school sophomore sitting on the edge of his seat and, suddenly, I had a vision.

In the Spirit I saw what looked like a little black monkey clinging to one of his lungs. Not wanting to alarm him or his family, I merely asked if he was having a problem with one of his lungs. His father immediately blurted out, "The doctors have just found tuberculosis on his left lung!"

Without hesitation I had him stand as I rebuked the spirit of tuberculosis. In the Spirit I saw that monkey-like creature drop to the ground and run out of the building. Before this series of meetings was over (I spoke every Sunday night there for nine weeks), the family came back from the doctor with the report that every trace of the tuberculosis had gone!

Standing in that church lobby nearly twenty years later, Joe told me that he had recently been in an automobile accident. During routine medical examinations to determine his injuries following the accident, the doctors x-rayed his lungs. He was still clean! There was still absolutely no trace of tuberculosis. Hallelujah!

I rejoiced to hear that Joe Delgado was still healed after all those years, but I was even more blessed to learn that he was pastoring his own church! He was attending that ministers' meeting because he was in the ministry! Not only had he been affected physically in those meetings in 1982, the Word of God had impacted his spirit. A fire was ignited in him that was still burning after all those years.

To see Joe walking in truth, doing something with what he heard, blessed me beyond measure! Though I am sure that many others were responsible for influencing him for Christ, I was pleased to know that I had at least a small part in planting the truth in Joe's heart.

3. You should surpass your father's success.

Responsibility number three for healthy spiritual children is surpassing your father's success.

> **"Then the Lord your God will bring you to the land which your fathers possessed, and you shall possess it. He will prosper you and multiply you more than your fathers."**
>
> **Deuteronomy 30:5**

This verse of Deuteronomy contains not only a physical promise for Israel, but also a spiritual principle for those being mentored by fathers in the Lord today. *The children shall possess that which their fathers possessed and be prospered and multiplied beyond their fathers.* This is not only a potential blessing to be enjoyed, but also a responsibility to be fulfilled.

A Christian who has been properly mentored should go beyond the success achieved by his spiritual father. The reason for this is simple: The one being mentored has the advantage of learning from the father's experience and wisdom, so it is not only beneficial that we listen to the wisdom of our fathers—it is essential!

Many times, more can be learned from people telling us what they did wrong than from what they did right. So a true father in the faith will not only share his victories with those under his wing, he will be careful to share his mistakes as well. It has been said, "You'd better learn from the mistakes of others because you don't have time to make them all yourself." I wholeheartedly agree.

Unfortunately, some have formed the habit of sharing their history by stringing all of their victories together—forgetting to mention their defeats and setbacks. The result is that many new Christians get an unrealistic picture of the Christian life and become discouraged when their experience doesn't measure up.

Thank God that as we read the stories in Scripture of our heroes of faith, we get a realistic picture of them—warts and all. We see men like Moses, Samson, David, Peter, and Paul doing exploits for God, but we also see them occasionally stumble and sin. God tells the whole story, and through it, we learn both what to do and what to avoid doing.

Whenever I can, I endeavor to share with other pastors—especially those starting out in the ministry—both my successes and my failures. If they will listen, l can save them a lot of time and heartache, because they have the advantage of learning not only from their own experience, but from mine as well.

Although we must walk within the parameters and boundaries of our individual callings, we should be wise enough not to fight all over again for the ground that our fathers possessed. We should inherit from them, learn from them, and then go on and possess more for the glory of our King in whatever particular ministry or field He has called us to. (2 Cor. 10:13.)

IMPORTANT PRECAUTIONS FOR SPIRITUAL FATHERS

Spiritual mentoring, like natural parenting, has its rewards—but it also has its pitfalls. It would be great to have all of the experiences associated with fatherhood and then be able to instruct and guide our children in the way they should go. But the inescapable truth is that, just as children haven't experienced being children before, neither have fathers experienced being fathers before. The inevitable result is that some mistakes are going to be made along the way. The purpose of this final chapter is to help minimize those mistakes by focusing on several areas where spiritual fathers most commonly miss the mark.

1. **Spiritual fathers must guard against becoming jealous if their children surpass their success.**

When Joseph told his father, Jacob, about the dream he had received in which the sun, moon, and eleven stars bowed down to him, Jacob rebuked him. His father recoiled instantly at the thought of Joseph becoming greater than he. But unlike Joseph's brothers, who utterly rejected the dream because of hateful jealousy, Jacob wisely kept the matter in mind. (Gen. 37:9-11.)

Unfortunately, Jacob's reaction is not an uncommon one. Many an aspiring prodigy has been stunned to see this same attitude manifested in the life of his or her mentor when he or she begins to excel. Some people will encourage and cheer you on *until you begin to do well.* Then, due to their own insecurity—feeling threatened by your success—they will either cut you off, or try to cut you down to size.

In reality, if one of your students does well, it is a reflection on you. It means that you have done your job well. When someone whom you have poured your life into begins to prosper and multiply beyond your personal experience, it should be cause for rejoicing. This is one of the goals of fathering.

A coach doesn't get jealous because his team wins first place! Their success is not only a reflection of the team members' ability and heart, it is a reflection of the coach's ability to coach! He shouldn't get jealous even if the team he coaches beats the record of the team he played on years before. A good coach realizes that when his players excel, their reward is his reward.

My oldest son, Harrison, has recently taken up the game of golf. He has been blessed with amazing athletic ability, so it didn't take him long to excel at the game. Though he is new to the game and I've been playing golf for many years, I am finding it more and more difficult to beat him. In fact, I have already resigned myself to the inevitable: It won't be long until I will be the one doing the chasing instead of him.

Will I be angry when the day comes that Harrison can soundly thrash me on a golf course? Will I become jealous and refuse to play with him or forbid him to practice?

No, of course not. He is my son, and I'm teaching him everything I know about the game so he can excel. His victory is my victory. His success, in part, will be a reflection on me. I want him to do well. I expect him to be better than I, and I am doing all that I can to ensure his success on the golf course—but, more importantly, in the game of life.

2. Fathers must tend to their own spiritual growth.

It is not an option to stop growing in spiritual life. As believers, we never fully arrive at spiritual maturity. We must always strive to "...become more and more in every way like Christ..." (Eph. 4:15 TLB). The apostle Paul declares in Philippians: Not that I have already attained, or am already perfected; but I press on" (Phil. 3:12).

Spiritual fathers must take this business of "pressing on" seriously. If they don't, even the things that once burned brightly in their hearts can slip away.

> **Only take heed to thyself, and keep thy soul diligently, lest thou forget the things which thine eyes have seen, and lest they depart from thy heart all the days of thy life: but teach them thy sons, and thy sons' sons.**
>
> **Deuteronomy 4:9 KJV**

If the father doesn't take heed to guard himself and keep (protect, tend, and care for) his spiritual life (his soul and spirit), it is possible that the things which once lived and flourished in his heart can depart. If that happens, the father can't carry out his God-given assignment of transferring those spiritual treasures to the following generations.

In many ways, growing in God is like a fish swimming upstream. Although at times more effort is needed to ascend the steeper places, the fish doesn't look at it as an impossibility or as an unfair demand. He is made for the water. God has given him all the equipment he needs to swim upstream. It is completely natural to him. But if he ever decides to stop making progress or to stop *facing upstream*, he will immediately forfeit his position and be swept back downstream by the water's currents.

In a spiritual parallel, God's children have been equipped with all we need for our spiritual journey in Christ. Growing in God is natural for the Christian. Granted, sometimes the steep places can be difficult, but we were created to succeed, and we can make it.

But whenever a child of God stops *facing upstream* and ceases to press on, he or she will immediately begin to lose ground, being swept downstream by the currents of the world.

Paul encourages Timothy along these lines as he speaks to him about fulfilling the role of a mentor:

> **Let no one despise your youth, but be an example to the believers in word, in conduct, in love, in spirit, in faith, in purity.**
>
> **Do not neglect the gift that is in you, which was given to you by prophecy with the laying on of the hands of the eldership. Meditate on these things; give yourself entirely to them, that your progress may be evident to all. Take heed to yourself and to the doctrine. Continue in them, for in doing this you will save both yourself and those who hear you.**
>
> **1 Timothy 4:12,14-16**

God expects us to make progress. If we are to serve as examples, it is essential that we continue forward daily. Yes, the stream will try to push us back, but we can conquer it. The father who doesn't tend to his own spiritual growth will one day discover that he has nothing more to give.

Years ago I went with some friends to visit a man who had been used by God to lead a great revival at one time. The city where he lived and ministered was shaken for the gospel. A great awakening had taken place because of his obedience. I was so excited (and a little nervous) at the thought of getting to meet someone who had walked so close to God and had so much to share.

This man had retired from ministry many years before and now lived in a large house in the country. As we drove up, I could feel my anticipation mounting.

What marvelous stories were waiting to be told?

What great words of wisdom would be shared?

We were invited into the house and ushered into the study where he sat. Our meeting that day had a deep impact on me, but not in the way I had expected. Instead of swimming in a "well of wisdom," listening to him was more like shuffling through a dried-up riverbed. I was hoping to leave encouraged and inspired to do exploits for God. Instead, I left discouraged and a bit confused.

Here was a man who had been mightily used by God. He had seen scores of people saved, witnessed miracles, and yet all he had to say was, "Don't get too carried away with ideas of doing things for God or with thoughts of seeing a move of God's Spirit."

And he made sure we didn't leave without realizing how many mistakes he felt were in the *King James Version* of the Bible. That meeting had a lasting impact on me, but it wasn't a positive one—except for the fact that I prayed I would never end up like that myself: cynical and reclusive with the curtains drawn over the windows of life. This once great man had ceased to progress and had lost much of the precious treasure God had entrusted him with to pass on to the next generation.

3. Fathers must guard against becoming dictatorial.

The aim of a true mentor in the faith is to help mold his spiritual offspring into servants of Christ—not servants of the mentor. There are some who, in the name of providing spiritual leadership, have begun to dominate those entrusted to their care—and this is something God never intended.

Bringing your children to a place of spiritual maturity does not include fostering in them a perpetual dependence on yourself. Though all believers have a need to be connected to a local church, it is not God's plan that His people be in bondage to individual leaders. In this kind of unbiblical relationship, "underlings" are required to look to their leader before making even the smallest decisions.

Some years ago in America, there was a movement which, I believe, had the importance of mentoring at its core. But unfortunately, that truth was taken to an erroneous extreme in some circles. Many leaders recognized the need for believers to be individually mentored. They witnessed the same lack of spiritual fathers in the body of Christ today that Paul declared existed in his day. So in an attempt to help fill this need, they set up a system in which someone older and more mature in the Lord could mentor individual Christians.

But things eventually came crashing down when some of the foundational leaders began to espouse rigid control of those under their care. Things became so extreme that in some cases the people being mentored were not allowed to make even the smallest decisions without first checking with their leaders. It became more of a dictator/servant relationship than a father/son relationship.

A friend of mine in ministry experienced the same thing. He was a new Christian and soon began attending a local church in his area. He met a young lady who had been raised in the church, and they fell in love and married. Things went well for a while until he began to question why some of the church leaders were allowed to wield so much influence in their personal lives.

They were taught both publicly and privately that they were to submit all decisions to church leadership for approval. That included where they could live, what automobile they were allowed to buy, what job they could take, and even how they spent their leisure time.

My friend said it became a nightmare. Every area of their lives, down to the smallest detail, was being controlled by church leaders. After voicing his disagreement, he was told that he was "rebellious" and needed "to get in line."

Finding no relief, he finally decided to leave that church, but, sadly, his wife wouldn't leave with him. She had grown up there, and their whole way of thinking had been so ingrained in her that she couldn't see the obvious error. The church leadership insisted that she divorce her husband, which she promptly did.

Devastated and confused, my friend suddenly found himself without a wife or a church, and was very unclear on how God-ordained leadership was supposed to function. It was only by the grace of God that he recovered from this ordeal, and today, he is again serving the Lord.

Without question, God both calls and establishes leaders in His church, giving them the responsibility and authority to oversee His work. In harmony with that, God also calls all believers to be a part of and submit to a local church and its pastoral leadership. But the object of God's government is to help people mature in Christ and release them to fulfill their destiny, not to subdue and subjugate them—keeping them on a short leash or under a lid.

God wants His leaders to lead by example—not by dictate. Peter makes this truth profoundly clear in his address to a group of elders (spiritual fathers) in 1 Peter 5:1-3:

> **The elders who are among you I exhort, I who am a fellow elder and a witness of the sufferings of Christ, and also a partaker of the glory that will be revealed: shepherd the flock of God which is among you, serving as overseers, not by compulsion but willingly, not for dishonest gain but eagerly; nor as being lords over those entrusted to you, but being examples to the flock.**

May we follow Peter's admonition and endeavor to lead by example. After all, our lives speak louder than our lips, and our ways are more persuasive than our words will ever be.

4. Spiritual fathers must endeavor to never judge their children by outward appearance.

Don't sell people short as to what God might do in and through them based on outward appearance. It has been my experience over the course of several decades of ministry that, many times, God uses the most unlikely vessels. He regularly uses people who most thought would never amount to anything to accomplish His purposes. That way He gets all the glory.

When Samuel went to Bethlehem to anoint a new king from among Jesse's sons, David wasn't even called to the gathering. He was the youngest and was left with the task of tending his father's sheep.

When Samuel saw Jesse's eldest son, Eliab, He said, "Surely the Lord's anointed is before Him" (1 Sam. 16:6). But God's response reveals an eternal truth that we need to embrace. "But the Lord said to Samuel, 'Do not look at his appearance or at his physical stature, because I have refused him. For the Lord does not see as man sees; for man looks at the outward appearance, but the Lord looks at the heart'" (v. 7).

After this, seven of Jesse's sons were made to pass before Samuel, and God rejected all of them. Samuel had to ask Jesse, "Are all the young men here?" Apparently, it had never even crossed Jesse's mind that his son David might be the one whom God had chosen.

History tells the rest. David went on to be Israel's greatest king, one of the Bible's most beloved characters and the writer of most of the book of Psalms, which has provided guidance and comfort to millions of people throughout the centuries. This is quite a legacy from the forgotten son out tending the sheep.

I had an interesting experience shortly after my conversion to Christ. I had spent some time talking with a local Christian leader, along with a friend of mine who was not yet saved. The man we spoke with was one of the most influential Christians in town. He was the dean of the only Christian academy in the largest church in our area.

After our meeting, this leader sought out the person who was mentoring me and shared this advice: "Don't waste your time on Bayless. He's hopeless. It would be an effort in futility to try and do something with him. He'll never amount to anything." Then he added, "The wisest thing you could do would be to spend your time sowing into the life of his friend. He has real potential."

I was sure glad the individual helping me chose to ignore that advice. To date, my friend has never served God a day of his life, but my story, obviously, has turned out a bit differently.

Why would someone give that kind of counsel in the first place? Because he judged me based on outward appearances. You might have been tempted to do the same. You see, at that time I hadn't had a haircut in more than seven years. I had a long beard and sometimes would wear a long braid down the side of my head with a feather or some other ornament tied to the end.

My clothes were a bit tattered, and I just didn't have the look of someone who was going places with God. But God knew my heart, and He was faithful to show it to a few others who encouraged me along the way.

As we assume the role of a father in Christ, let us be prayerful and careful not to sell our children short, remembering that "God has chosen the foolish things of the world to put to shame the wise, and God has chosen the weak things of the world to put to shame the things which are mighty; and the base things of the world and the things which are despised God has chosen, and the things which are not, to bring to nothing the things that are, that no flesh should glory in His presence" (1 Cor. 1:27-29).

5. Spiritual fathers must be careful not to invest in people's lives for the motive of personal benefit.

In writing to the same group of people whom he had called his children in the Lord, the apostle Paul says:

> Now for the third time I am ready to come to you. And I will not be burdensome to you; for I do not seek yours, but you. For the children ought not to lay up for the parents, but the parents for the children. And I will very gladly spend and be spent for

your souls; though the more abundantly I love you, the less I am loved.

2 Corinthians 12:14,15

Paul was telling his spiritual children that he wasn't investing into them for what he might get out of them. In fact, he basically told them, "If you never reciprocate and return my love, if I never personally benefit from my labors among you, I will gladly continue on. My purpose is not to get something from you, but to give something to you."

How different this is from some who claim to be spiritual fathers today. The popular doctrine among many seems to be that the children are obligated to lay up for the parents, and this is the exact opposite of what Scripture teaches. (Prov. 13:22.) It is a sad thing to see leaders in the church making merchandise of their followers. (2 Peter 2:3 KJV.)

"But," you say, "won't God bless those who endeavor to bless and give into the lives of God's servants?"

Yes, without question. But the difficulty arises when God's servants only serve with such an anticipated blessing in mind—or, worse yet, when proclaimed "spiritual fathers" demand that their children bless them monetarily and in other ways. Too many behind the pulpit and on TV declare this is the only way their spiritual children will reap rich blessings in their own lives, and such doctrine is dangerous. It strikes at the very heart of true spiritual fatherhood.

While I was still a Bible school student, I was invited by another student to lead worship in a church meeting at which he had been invited to preach. He told me in glowing terms how much my guitar playing and singing would add to the service and that he felt led to ask me to accompany him on the trip.

I was imagining how great it would be to have the opportunity to minister in song, when my thoughts were shattered by his next statement: "Oh! And, by the way, I need you to drive because I don't have a car."

Reality hit with a thud as I realized his motive for including me in his ministry opportunity hadn't been my musical talents, but something else he needed that I had—a car. Asking to borrow my car in the first place, rather than trying to manipulate me into using it, would have been preferable.

This kind of maneuvering in a young Bible school student may be excusable, but not when it comes from one claiming to be a spiritual father. True spiritual fathers pour their lives into their children, regardless of whether it is personally reciprocated, and without regard to whether there will be potential material benefit. If the children reciprocate, wonderful! They will be abundantly blessed for it. But someone who will only mentor others for a guaranteed payback has missed the Father's heart.

Some time ago, a dear friend of mine, who pastors one of America's great churches, shared with me that he was told by someone that if he stopped financially supporting a certain minister (whom we both looked to as a father in the faith), that he would immediately be "cut off." If the money stopped flowing in, this "father in the faith" would never again "give him the time of day."

I remember thinking to myself, *There is no way. This man doesn't think that way. He isn't sowing into us just because of the money his ministry gets from us.* (I was supporting this ministry as well.)

My friend decided to test the waters, so to speak. He didn't send his regular monthly offering for a few months (he had previously given huge sums of money to this man's ministry) and waited to see what would happen.

Both of us were utterly astonished at what transpired. As predicted, this "father in the faith" immediately dropped all relations with my friend. Suddenly, he was treated as though he never existed. Except for one query as to whether he was going to give any more money (my friend was told it was the only way their relationship was going to continue), no other contact was ever initiated.

This, quite obviously, was a tragedy—not so much for us as young ministers—but more for the loss of a great father who could have left an even greater legacy had he not fallen prey to this kind of error in his later years.

God, beyond all argument, has promised to bless us when we bless others. We cannot sow into the lives of others without reaping rich rewards in our own lives. The unalterable spiritual law is that "...whatever a man sows, that he will also reap" (Gal. 6:7).

Let us learn to rest in that, being confident that God keeps perfect records. Nothing escapes His scrutinizing gaze. He will repay every good deed and every act of love, "...good measure, pressed down, shaken together, and running over..." (Luke 6:38). Granted, payday may not come on the first of every month with God, but it always comes. Believe it. Expect it. And keep on "laying up for the children."

6. Spiritual fathers must realize that spiritual children never outgrow the need for their prayers.

Paul makes a statement that amounts to a lifelong consecration to pray for his spiritual offspring in Galatia: *My little children, for whom I labor in birth again until Christ is formed in you* (Gal. 4:19).

Paul had labored for them in birth (pictorial language for laboring in prayer) since he had first shared the gospel with them, leading them to Christ. And now he says that he is laboring in birth again until Christ is formed in them.

My friend, that is a lifelong process. As long as we are breathing, God's Spirit will continually be taking us "...from glory to glory"... (2 Cor. 3:18). We will continually be going "...from faith to faith..." (Rom. 1:17).

The forming of Christ in us will never be complete as long as we live in these temples of clay. So Paul, in essence, was echoing the fact that no matter how mature we become, we never outgrow our need for prayer.

Look at what Paul writes to Timothy, his beloved son in the faith: "I thank God, whom I serve with a pure conscience, as my forefathers did, as without ceasing I remember you in my prayers night and day" (2 Tim. 1:3).

Even the great apostle himself solicited the prayers of the saints on numerous occasions: "Now I beg you, brethren, through the Lord Jesus Christ, and through the love of the Spirit, that you strive together with me in prayers to God for me" (Rom. 15:30).

"Brethren, pray for us" (1 Thess. 5:25).

"Finally, brethren, pray for us..." (2 Thess. 3:1).

"...I trust that through your prayers I shall be granted to you" (Philem. 22).

If Paul felt the need to be prayed for, with as much knowledge and experience as he had, it should be obvious that all of us have a need for prayer. It is something we will never outgrow.

We recently held a prayer seminar in our church with a visiting minister whom I highly esteem in the Lord. He is known as a man of prayer. The first time he was with us, I requested to have an hour of prayer with him. As we sat in my office and prayed, I quite literally prayed with my eyes open. I wanted to observe this man as he engaged in conversation with the Master. It was a profound experience for me, and I learned some things that aided me in my own prayer life.

On the occasion of his return to our church, I was thrilled and humbled to learn that he had prayed for my wife and me daily since our last meeting more than two years earlier. Some might think as they observe Janet and me leading a successful church, television ministry, and other outreaches that send the gospel around the world: *They don't need prayer. They're already successful.*

On the contrary, both of us are deeply aware of our need for prayer. We are constantly in need of God's wisdom and strength. In fact, if you would, take a moment right now and pray for us (unless this book has long outlived us) or for some other leaders in the body of Christ whom you know. The prayers of a person right with God make much power available, according to James 5:16.

7.   Realize that there is no retirement for spiritual fathers.

As you continue to grow in Christ and become a spiritual father or even a grandparent (seeing your spiritual offspring bring others to the Lord), you never reach a plateau where you can sit back and say, "My work is done. I think I'm going to retire." There is no retirement for the spiritually mature! As long as you are drawing breath, still living in this earth suit we call a body, your job is not over.

Naturally speaking, many people look forward to retirement. And generally, at least in America's culture, retirement is associated with the joy of spending time with the grandkids, whether it be for an occasional weekend or just for the day.

However, at the end of the appointed time, the grandkids are sent back to Mom and Dad, and Grandpa and Grandma no longer have to deal with all the pressures of parenting. They've had their turn. Now it's somebody else's.

Although this is a common experience in American culture, it's not in the culture of the gospel. There is no such thing as "now it's somebody else's turn" in the kingdom of God, at least when it comes to sharing Christ and seeing new babes born into God's family. Our responsibility in that arena lasts for the duration of our sojourn here.

In Genesis 23, Abraham's wife Sarah dies. After mourning Sarah's death, Abraham marries again, this time to a woman named

Keturah. He then proceeds to sire six more children. (Gen. 25:1,2.) The amazing thing is that when Abraham remarried, he was nearly 140 years old! That's the way God wants us to be when it comes to producing spiritual offspring. You are never too old to bring someone to Christ. In fact, the older you are in the Lord, the more you have to share with those who have newly come to the Father. No retirement. No checking out. If you have a pulse, you have a job to do. "The righteous shall flourish like a palm tree, he shall grow like a cedar in Lebanon. Those who are planted in the house of the Lord shall flourish in the courts of our God. They shall still bear fruit in old age; they shall be fresh and flourishing" (Ps. 92:12-14).

Perhaps you feel as I once did. You lament the fact that there are so few spiritual fathers and mothers in the church today. Let me challenge you with the words that challenged me: "It's time for you to stop looking for a father in the Lord and start being one."

May God richly bless you as you begin raising sons and daughters in the Lord. I know He will.

If you are new in the Lord and are looking for a spiritual father, find a good, Spirit-filled, Bible-believing church. Ask the Lord to bear witness through the Holy Spirit's leading as to where you are supposed to plant yourself; then stay there and grow!

In His grip,

Bayless Conley

ENDNOTES

Chapter 2

[1]*The New Compact Bible Dictionary*, p. 15, s.v. "Abraham."

[2]Barker, p. 19, s.v. "Abraham."

[3]*The New Compact Bible Dictionary*, p. 525, s.v. "Sarai."

[4]Webster, p. 559, s.v. "gaze."

Chapter 5

[1]Strong, "Greek," p. 46, entry #3143, s.v. "marturomai."

[2]Strong, "Greek," p. 55, entry #3888, s.v. "paramutheomai."

Chapter 8

[1]Strong, "Hebrew," p. 54, entry #3513, s.v. "honor."

REFERENCES

Barker, William P. *Everyone in the Bible*. Westwood: Fleming H. Revell Company, 1966.

The New Compact Bible Dictionary. Grand Rapids: Regency Reference Library, an imprint of Zondervan Publishing House, 1967.

Strong, James. *Strong's Exhaustive Concordance of the Bible*, "Hebrew and Chaldee Dictionary," "Greek Dictionary of the New Testament." Nashville: Abingdon, 1890.

Webster's New World College Dictionary, 3rd ed. New York: Simon & Schuster, Inc., 1996.

ABOUT THE AUTHOR

God's call on Bayless Conley's life is to take a living Jesus to a dying world, and he has done exactly that—to anyone who would listen—since he received Christ as his Savior in 1973. He graduated from Rhema Bible Training Center in Tulsa, Oklahoma, in 1979 and accepted his first ministry position as an associate pastor for a small church in Beaumont, California. From the start, he made it clear to the senior pastor that he would eventually leave to start his own church in Los Alamitos, the city where he was raised.

With the blessing of his pastor, Bayless and his wife, Janet, soon began "Faith Bible Study" at the home of a relative in Los Alamitos. The mid-week meeting began with eight people and grew to twenty-five in a short time. When the congregation grew to sixty-five, Bayless and Janet rented a storefront and started Cottonwood Christian Center.

Today Cottonwood Christian Center is one of the fastest-growing churches in the Los Angeles basin. With two Saturday night services, four Sunday services, and one service on Wednesday each week, Pastor Conley ministers to approximately 4,600 people.

His annual "Outpouring" conferences attract standing-room-only crowds each November, and his television program, *Truth for Today with Bayless Conley*, has an expanding U.S. and world market, including KCAL in Los Angeles and the *Fox Family Channel* nationwide. The program is carried in Europe, Africa, India, Australia, Hong Kong, and many affiliate stations. He has also appeared as a guest on Trinity Broadcasting Network's Praise the Lord program, where he shared his testimony in-depth before a potential viewing audience of 35 million cable TV homes.

Bayless has published four books: *Turning Mistakes Into Miracles, Ten Marks of a False Minister, How to Make the Devil's Schemes Backfire,* and *Cast Down, But Not Destroyed.*

Bayless and Janet Conley make their home in Los Alamitos, California, and are the parents of three children.

To contact Bayless Conley

write:

Cottonwood Christian Center

P.O. Box 417

Los Alamitos, California 90720

Please include your prayer requests

and comments when you write.

Additional copies of this book
are available from your local bookstore.

HARRISON HOUSE
Tulsa, Oklahoma 74153

PRAYER OF SALVATION

A born-again, committed relationship with God is the key to the victorious life. Jesus, the Son of God, laid down His life and rose again so that we could spend eternity with Him in heaven and experience His absolute best on earth. The Bible says, "For God so loved the world, that he gave his only begotten Son, that whosoever believeth in him should not perish, but have everlasting life" (John 3:16).

It is the will of God that everyone receive eternal salvation. The way to receive this salvation is to call upon the name of Jesus and confess Him as your Lord. The Bible says, "That if thou shalt confess with thy mouth the Lord Jesus, and shalt believe in thine heart that God hath raised him from the dead, thou shalt be saved. For whosoever shall call upon the name of the Lord shall be saved" (Rom. 10:9,13).

Jesus has given salvation, healing, and countless benefits to all who call upon His name. These benefits can be yours if you receive Him into your heart by praying this prayer.

Father, I come to you right now as a sinner. Right now, I choose to turn away from sin, and I ask you to cleanse me of all unrighteousness. I believe that Your Son, Jesus, died on the cross to take away my sins. I also believe that He rose again from the dead so that I may be justified and made righteous through faith in Him. I call upon the name of Jesus Christ for salvation. I want Him to be the Savior and Lord of my life. Jesus, I choose to follow You, and I ask that You fill me with the power of the Holy Spirit. I declare that right now I am a born-again child of God. I am free from sin and full of the righteousness of God. I am saved in Jesus' name. Amen.

If you have prayed this prayer to receive Jesus Christ into your life, we would like to hear from you. Please write us at:

HARRISON HOUSE

P.O. Box 35035

Tulsa, Oklahoma 74153

You can also visit us on the web at

www.harrisonhouse.com

THE HARRISON HOUSE VISION

Proclaiming the truth and the power
Of the Gospel of Jesus Christ
With excellence;

Challenging Christians to
Live victoriously,
Grow spiritually,
Know God intimately.